The Story Luke Tells

The Story Luke Tells

Luke's Unique Witness to the Gospel

Justo L. González

William B. Eerdmans Publishing Company
Grand Rapids, Michigan / Cambridge, U.K.

WM. B. EERDMANS PUBLISHING CO.

2140 Oak Industrial Drive N.E., Grand Rapids, Michigan 49505 /

P.O. Box 163, Cambridge CB3 9PU U.K.

www.eerdmans.com

Printed in the United States of America

21 20 19 18 17 16 15   7 6 5 4 3 2 1

Library of Congress Cataloging-in-Publication Data

González, Justo L.
The story Luke tells: Luke's unique witness to the gospel /
Justo L. González.
pages   cm
ISBN 978-0-8028-7200-5 (pbk.: alk. paper)
1. Bible. Luke — Criticism, interpretation, etc.
2. Bible. Acts — Criticism, interpretation, etc.   I. Title.

BS2589.G66   2015
226.4′06 — dc23

2014033462

Unless otherwise noted, the Scripture quotations in this publication are from
the New Revised Standard Version Bible, copyright © 1989 by the Division
of Christian Education of the National Council of Churches of Christ in the
U.S.A., and used by permission.

Contents

Introduction

A MONG ALL THE WRITERS of the New Testament, no one has been more undervalued than Luke. If most of us were asked to name the two main writers of the New Testament, we would probably say that they were Paul and John. But even by the simple measure of the extensiveness of their writings, this is not true. The Bible with which I am working now devotes 62 pages to the epistles of Paul — including among them those writings that most scholars consider deutero-Pauline. This Bible devotes 45 pages to the Johannine writings — and in this case, too, it is highly unlikely that the same author produced all of them. But this same Bible devotes 66 pages to the two writings by the single author whom we call Luke: the Third Gospel and the book of Acts.

While Luke is important for the extensiveness of his work, he is even more important for its content. The book of Acts has no parallel in the New Testament. Some of Paul's epistles — for instance, Colossians and Ephesians — resemble each other. But Acts is a unique book, for almost everything that it says cannot be found elsewhere in the New Testament. And, even though it clearly is parallel to Matthew and Mark, the Gospel of Luke also has much content that is unique to it. Its narrative of the infancy and youth of Jesus appears in neither Matthew nor Mark. As we shall see further on, Luke's genealogy of Jesus is much more far-reaching than the one in Matthew.

In the Gospel of Luke we find several episodes that either are much abbreviated in the other Gospels or do not appear at all in them — among others, the stories of Mary and Martha, the ten lepers, and Zacchaeus; Jesus' prediction of the destruction of Jerusalem and his trial before Herod; and the appearance of Jesus on the road to Emmaus, the apparition of Jesus in Jerusalem, and Jesus' ascension. Likewise, several of the most famous parables of Jesus are known only because of the witness of Luke — among others, the parables of the Good Samaritan, the neighbor who arrives late at night asking for bread for an unexpected visitor, the foolish rich man, the prodigal son, the unfaithful steward, Lazarus and the rich man, and the unjust judge. And these are only a few of the many differences between the Gospel of Luke and the other Gospels, for at every turn we find that Luke presents things in a different way. For instance, when we compare the Beatitudes in Matthew with those in Luke, we note that he also adds a series of woes.

All of this means that, while Luke shares the faith of the other Evangelists and of Paul, his understanding of that faith reflects his own perspective, that there are certain subjects that Luke underscores, and that therefore his perspective and his theology merit specific consideration similar to that given to Paul when his thought is compared with that of the Evangelists or other authors in the New Testament. Thus the purpose of this brief book is to investigate and expound something of Luke's theology, underlining both those elements which he shares with the rest of the New Testament authors and those which are unique to him.

If we then ask "Who is this Luke who wrote such an extensive portion of the New Testament?" we immediately have to acknowledge that on this point Paul has the advantage over Luke. We know about Paul through his epistles, through the book of Acts — actually written by Luke — and through other witnesses in ancient Christian literature. Of Luke we know no more than what can be discovered in his two writings, the Gospel and Acts, and this is not much.

It is often suggested that the author of the Third Gospel and Acts is the same Luke to whom Paul refers in Colossians 4:14 as

"Luke, the beloved physician." The same name appears again at the end of the epistle to Philemon, where Paul sends greetings from Epaphras, who is his companion in prison for Christ Jesus, as well as from Mark, Aristarchus, Demas, and Luke, "my fellow workers." In 2 Timothy 4:11 we are presented with Paul declaring that "only Luke is with me." Therefore, there is no doubt that among the companions and collaborators of Paul, there was a certain Luke, who was a physician.

What is in doubt is that this Luke, "the beloved physician," is the same author of the Third Gospel and of Acts. In ancient times, when somebody wrote a book — and especially when it was dedicated to a specific person, as is the case with the two books by Luke, which are addressed to Theophilus — seldom was the book given a title. Therefore, most likely the Third Gospel and Acts were known to the first readers as "the first book to Theophilus" and "the second book to Theophilus." But from a very early date — and certainly in the most ancient manuscripts preserved — it was affirmed that both of these books were written by Luke, Paul's companion. Towards the end of the second century, the distinguished bishop Irenaeus of Lyon, one of the most important Christian leaders of his time, simply confirmed it. At about the same time, or shortly thereafter, the document known as the "Muratorian Canon" says likewise. And even before Irenaeus, the chief heretic Marcion, whose teachings other Christians rejected, affirmed that the Gospel of Luke was written by Paul's companion.

Marcion thought that there was a marked contrast and even contraposition between the God of the Old Testament and that of the New, who is superior to the former. He therefore took the epistles of Paul, expunged from them every quotation or reference to the Old Testament and every positive word regarding the Law of Israel, and declared these epistles to be his sacred scripture. He likewise took the Gospel of Luke, took out from it everything that he deemed "Judaized," and declared that, since Luke had been a companion of Paul, it was his Gospel that most faithfully interpreted the Pauline message, and therefore, this book — jointly with Paul's letters — should be the only sacred scripture for true believers in the Father of Jesus Christ.

Thus, there is no doubt that by the middle of the second century, the universal opinion of orthodox believers as well as of Marcionites was that the author of these two books was the same Luke to whom Paul refers in his epistles. According to Paul himself, Luke was a physician. This seems to be corroborated by several medical references that appear in Luke's two books, although it is also true that such references were relatively common, and do not prove that their author was a physician — just as the fact that somebody speaks of "sinusitis" or of "neuralgia" does not mean that the person is a physician.

There is, however, another sign that the author of these books was a companion of Paul. Toward the end of the book of Acts there are long passages written in the first-person plural — "we" — in contrast with the rest of the book, which is mostly written in the third person — Paul went, preached, traveled, and so on — or in the third-person plural — they went, they said, and so on. Although some scholars doubt this point, the use of the "we" form would seem to indicate that the author was among those who were traveling with Paul.

There is one final point that may be brought to bear on the question of the authorship of these books. In Acts 13 we are given a list of the leaders in the church in Antioch: Barnabas, Simeon who was also called Niger, Lucius of Cyrene, Manaen, and Saul. The name "Lucius" may be a variant of "Luke," and therefore it is possible that the Lucius of Acts 13 is the same Luke of Colossians and Philemon. There certainly is no doubt that the author of Acts knew the church in Antioch quite well, as well as its history and its missionary labors. All of this leads some to think that the Lucius of Cyrene that Acts mentions is the author both of that book itself and of the previous volume, the Gospel of Luke. In that case, there is another detail that we know about Luke: he was from Cyrene, on the north coast of Africa. It is interesting to note that in the list this Lucius of Cyrene appears next to a certain Simeon who is called "Niger" — that is to say, "Simeon the black man." Since many of the inhabitants of North Africa were of dark complexion, they were often called "Niger." Could it be then that this Simeon of Niger is the same who appears in the Gospel as Simon of Cyrene? And since Lucius was also from Cyrene, is it possible that he also was dark-skinned? And, if Lucius is the same as Luke, will it then turn out to be that this author, the most prolific in the entire New Testament, was of dark complexion? It is impossible to affirm it as a fact, but it is still a possibility. . . .

This seems to be all that can be known or even guessed about the life of this ancient brother in the faith who over the centuries has had such an enormous impact on the church.

But we do know more. We know that, no matter who he was, and no matter where he came from, he has left us two books that help us understand both the message of the gospel of Jesus Christ and the thought and interests of Luke himself. Like others before him — and countless others after him — Luke proposes to tell the story of Jesus. And like every one of those others, he has his own interests, perspectives, and emphases. Therefore, much of what Luke has to tell us today in the midst of our own situation and interests has to do with his perspective and emphases. It is therefore important to consider some of those emphases and interests, which certainly help us today to draw nearer to Luke's Master and ours.

ONE

Luke and the History of Humankind

Many have undertaken to set down an orderly account
of the events that have been fulfilled among us.
Luke 1:1

SINCE I MYSELF AM a historian, I am quite interested in this dimension of Luke's work. However, this is not just a matter of my own personal interest, but also of the interests of our time. Just reading the newspapers or watching the news on television shows us that our generation is captivated by the theme of history. But this is not history as it used to be studied in school — a series of facts, names, battles, rulers, and dates. Rather, it is history as the context of all of life. The history that I studied as a child was presented as having to do only with the past. Today, the history that interests us is also about the present and how it will inform the future. Politicians study history in order to refer to past moments which may serve to ground their present activities and goals. Thus, in Latin America some say that they are "Bolivarianos," others that they are "Martianos," and still others that they are "Sandinistas." In each of those cases, people are referring to the past — to Simón Bolívar, José Martí, and Augusto Sandino. But it is not just a matter of the past, for the past one chooses and the manner in which it is interpreted may be a matter of life and death for many in the present. Another example would be the issue of immigrants in the United States. When discussing immigration, some compare it with the invasion of the Roman Empire by the Germanic peoples, who slowly moved into the lands of the Empire until the time came when the Empire itself was overwhelmed and eventually disappeared. But there are others who point out that the United States itself is basically a nation of immigrants, and also point out that many of the ancestors of today's citizens entered the country without any documents. In short, each side of the debate chooses a particular moment in history and interprets it in such a way that it bolsters its own current position.

These examples clearly show that in the final analysis we have no more valuable resource for facing the present than the past. This morning I knew that the sun would rise because every morning for many centuries the sun has risen. Without that history, I would not have the slightest idea when or if the day would begin. Today, when people debate how to solve the problem of budget deficits in their nations and suggest various solutions, the only basis they have to defend their proposals is history, the experience of what happened in the past when certain measures were taken or certain events took place. Therefore, history, although focusing its attention on the past, is above all a matter of the present.

History is also a matter of the future. In the above-mentioned debate about national deficits, people often refer to the future. What will happen to our children and our grandchildren if we do not solve the problem now? At a personal level, when we tell our children to study so that they may have a good future, the only argument we have is that in the past those who studied usually found a way towards a more promising future. Thus we say to them that if they study, they will be able to become doctors or scientists or lawyers. On an entirely different level, Fidel Castro was also referring to that future history when, after being convicted as a terrorist by a Cuban court, he claimed, "History will absolve me." In short, without history the present would be like a deep cave without any light. The future would be like a series of high ledges within that cave, where we would risk falling at every step. That is the reason why history — both past and present — is of such great interest today. But there is also a widespread ignorance of history today. A young man who is sitting on a park bench and sending a text to a friend is very much aware that he lives in unprecedented circumstances, but he forgets that the technologies that have led to his ability to send a text message did not fall down from heaven last year, but have a long history that took centuries and even millennia of discoveries, theories, errors, and inventions.

Unfortunately, many Christians are like that young man on the bench. We imagine that the Bible came to us by falling down directly from heaven. We forget the centuries it took to write it. We forget the thousands of believers who carefully copied it once and again. We forget the translators who have made it accessible to us in our own language. In short, we forget the great multitude of believers that no one could count who connect us with Isaiah, with Paul, with Luke, and with Jesus. In forgetting, we miss much of the richness of the Bible itself, just as the young man sending a text in the park forgets the long history making this possible, and therefore is unable to appreciate the true value of his phone.

It is precisely that need to connect with the past that lies at the center of Luke's work. As he says to Theophilus, his purpose in writing is "so that you may know the truth concerning the things about which you have been instructed" (Luke 1:4). This would seem to imply that Theophilus was already a believer. He did not need to be convinced of the truth of the gospel. But even so, Luke is convinced that in reading his story, Theophilus will attain a fuller understanding of what he already believes. Luke is connecting Theophilus with his past — with a past in which there probably is much that he does not know, but which is at the very foundation of his faith. Thus, we may conceive of the Third Gospel and the book of Acts as a golden chain with a series of links connecting

Theophilus with Jesus. And the building of such chains is precisely the task of all history.

*   *   *

But Luke is also interested in the order of his narrative. Significantly, he seems to be referring to other Gospel writers as those who "have undertaken to set down an orderly account of the events" (Luke 1:1). Even though at first reading this would seem to imply that Luke believes that his narrative will be better than those others, in fact Luke never says such a thing, but rather declares that "I too decided . . . to write an orderly account for you" (Luke 1:3; my emphasis). The word too is important, because with it Luke acknowledges the value of the work of others. He is not writing to correct them. He is writing a new history because he has a specific purpose: to make these things known to Theophilus — and, by implication, to the entire generation of Theophilus. The new history is based not on a different past, but on a specific present. The new history becomes necessary because the same events are being read from new perspectives. And this is something every historian knows.

But it is not only in this sense that Luke should be considered a historian. Among all the Evangelists, only Luke shows a particular interest in dating the events that he discusses. After his prologue or dedication to Theophilus, he begins his narrative by saying that these things occurred "in the days of King Herod of Judea" (Luke 1:5). This is the way that events were dated in ancient times. For instance, the prophet Isaiah gives us the date of his vision by declaring in chapter 6 of his book that it took place "in the year in which King Uzziah died," and in chapter 7 he gives a date for what he is about to tell by saying that it happened "in the days of Ahaz, son of Jotham, son of Uzziah, king of Judah" (Isa. 6:1; 7:1). In the

Apostles' Creed we say that Jesus "suffered under Pontius Pilate" — not to blame Pilate, but rather to date the passion of Jesus. Likewise, the reference to Herod at the beginning of the Gospel of Luke serves to date what Luke is about to tell us. Matthew also tells us that the birth of Jesus took place "in the days of King Herod" (Matt. 2:1). But Mark does not give us a date, and John, in the prologue to his work, begins his narrative by saying simply, "There was a man sent from God, whose name was John" (John 1:6). In contrast to Mark and John, and much more consistently than Matthew, Luke dates the events that he narrates. Among the many examples that could be given, let one suffice: compare Luke 3:1-2 with the parallel passage in Matthew 3:1. In both the author is introducing John the Baptist and his work. Matthew simply tells us, "In those days John the Baptist appeared." By contrast, Luke says, "In the fifteenth year of the reign of Emperor Tiberius, when Pontius Pilate was governor of Judea, and Herod was ruler of Galilee, and his brother Philip ruler of the region of Ituraea and Trachonitis, and Lysanias ruler of Abilene, during the high priesthood of Annas and Caiaphas, the word of God came to John." Thus, while Matthew is simply interested in the event itself, Luke also wants to date it exactly, so that the reader can relate it to other events that were taking place at the same time.

And there is more. Luke is also interested in placing what he tells within its social, political, and religious context. Several of the names that appear in the list just quoted will be important characters in the rest of the narrative — Pontius Pilate, Herod, Annas, and Caiaphas. They are not abstract persons whose only purpose is to date what is being told; they are a sign of the interplay between Jesus' ministry and its political, religious, and social context. Luke's Jesus is not an abstract religious personage who goes about the world preaching and doing miracles; he is a man of flesh and blood who, like all humans, lives within a variety of contexts that impact his life, and that he also impacts. This is particularly important because, as we shall see later on, Luke is very much interested in matters of power — those who have it and those who do not — and the manner in which the gospel relates to them.

For these reasons, Luke is very careful not only regarding the dates of what he tells us, but also the geographical and political contexts. Both in his Gospel and in Acts there are precise references to places and political offices. As for the places, while the other Evangelists say that Jesus returned "to his land," Luke says that he returned "to Nazareth." Likewise, in Acts many specific places are mentioned that the general public would probably not know, but which Luke gives as points of reference. Thus, for instance, as Paul and his companions are being taken to Rome, the ship in which they sail seeks refuge under the lee of the island of Crete, in the bay that Luke calls "Fair Havens." The Greek name that Luke gives that bay is *Kaloi Limenes*. Today there is on the southern side of Crete a bay that is still called by that name, and its position and shape are such that, as Luke tells us in his narrative, ships within it are exposed to the fury of winter winds.

Luke seems to be equally careful in matters of politics and the titles due various officers. For instance, only those who ruled senatorial provinces were called proconsuls, and Luke is quite exact in giving that title to those governors who had it, such as Sergius Paulus, proconsul of Cyprus (Acts 13:7) and much later to Gallio, proconsul of Achaia (Acts 18:12). Of the first of these two, we know no more than what Luke tells us. But we do know that Gallio was a brother of Seneca the philosopher and a friend of Nero, and that he ruled in Achaia from July of 51 to July of the following year. (The position of proconsul was usually held for a single year.) So, thanks to Luke's care in giving us the names of the political characters involved in the story, we are able to determine that what we are told in Acts 18:1-17 about the activities of

Paul in Corinth must have taken place toward the end of the year 51 or early in 52.

Furthermore, Luke is not afraid to depict the true character of political leaders, warts and all. Take, for instance, the Roman tribune Claudius Lysias, who goes to the temple to arrest Paul in the midst of a riot (Acts 21:26-36), and then learns that Paul is a Roman citizen. When the time comes to tell his superior what has taken place, Lysias inverts the order of events and claims that he went to the temple in order to save Paul, because he knew that he was a Roman citizen (Acts 23:27). Then governor Felix, to whom Lysias has sent Paul, simply delays matters, and Luke clearly declares that he did this because "he hoped that money would be given him by Paul" (Acts 24:26). Then Luke adds that when Paul had already spent two years in prison, Felix left the province, but left Paul in prison so that his successor, Porcius Festus, would take care of the matter (Acts 24:27). This was quite obviously illegal, for two years was the maximum time during which an accused individual could be detained without being taken to trial. Then, in contrast with what he has said about Felix, Luke describes Porcius Festus as an energetic and decisive person who rapidly intervened in Paul's case. This agrees with what we know of Porcius Festus from other sources.

On the social dimensions of his narrative, Luke is also quite clear. In his Gospel we repeatedly find indications that the Galileans were regarded askance by those from Judea. Likewise, we see frequent references to the poor and to the contrast between them and the rich. Look, for instance, at the parable of the rich man and Lazarus, which is not found in any of the other Gospels. In Acts, when Lysias arrests Paul, he deals roughly with him until Paul speaks in a rather refined Greek, which immediately lets Lysias know that Paul is not what he thought. He then asks Paul, "Do you know Greek? Then you are not the Egyptian who recently stirred up a revolt and led the four thousand assassins out into the wilderness?" (Acts 21:37-38). As still happens in our societies today, Paul is judged by the manner of his speech.

Luke is equally careful in referring to the various religious positions of the Jewish leaders. Even though on occasion Jesus attacks the Pharisees, Luke does speak repeatedly of worthy Pharisees, some of whom show an interest in the teachings of Jesus. And when Paul faces the council of the Jews, Luke tells us that the tensions between Pharisees and Sadducees resulted in a riot such that the authorities had to intervene. In Luke's narrative, Paul declares, "Brothers, I am a Pharisee, a son of Pharisees. I am on trial concerning the hope of the resurrection of the dead." And then Luke goes on to tell us that "when he said this, a dissension began between the Pharisees and the Sadducees, and the assembly was divided. (The Sadducees say that there is no resurrection . . .)" (Acts 23:6-8). The debate then grows heated, the Pharisees taking Paul's side, with the result that the tribune, "fearing that they would tear Paul to pieces," intervenes. Note that in this narrative, besides taking into account and explaining the disagreements between Pharisees and Sadducees, Luke also paints the political picture of Palestine as it actually was, for in the final analysis it is the Roman authorities who held power, and they intervened in order to stop the dissension within the council of the Jews.

So, to sum up this far: as a historian Luke takes care to present his narrative in an orderly fashion and also to take into account the political, social, and religious context in which it takes place.

⋆   ⋆   ⋆

But there are other interesting dimensions in Luke's vision as a historian. One of them is the wide scope of his history. This is clear when we compare Luke with the other two Synoptic Gospels,

Matthew and Mark. Mark makes no effort to place his narrative within the general historical context, but simply dives immediately into the story of Jesus. Without any preamble, his Gospel simply begins with these words: "The beginning of the good news of Jesus Christ the Son of God." Somewhat later, when Matthew wrote his Gospel, he certainly had Mark's on hand and followed its general outline. But his book begins very differently: "An account of the genealogy of Jesus the Messiah, the son of David, the son of Abraham." That genealogy begins with Abraham and leads to Jesus. Thus, Matthew is placing the history of Jesus within the entirety of the history of Israel. Years later, when Luke wrote his Gospel, he certainly had on hand the Gospel of Mark and also, if not that of Matthew, at least some common sources from which both he and Matthew drew. Like Matthew, Luke presents the genealogy of Jesus — although not at the very beginning of his work, but rather in chapter 3. Unlike Matthew's genealogy, Luke's genealogy moves not from father to son, but from son to father. But here is the most critical difference: the genealogy of Luke not only hearkens back to Abraham, but continues all the way back to Adam. This allows Luke to do two things. First of all, he is able to end his genealogy with the phrase "Adam, son of God" (Luke 3:38). Since in the earlier chapter Luke has made it very clear that Jesus is the son of God, in giving Adam the title "son of God," Luke is implying that in Jesus a new creation begins. This theme of Jesus as the new Adam, as the beginning of a new creation, is typical of the theology that was beginning to develop around Antioch and Asia Minor at that time, and may be particularly seen in the writings of both Luke and Paul.

Luke's hearkening back to Adam allows him to do a second significant thing. When Matthew presents his genealogy, which ends with Abraham, he implies that Jesus is the culmination of the entire history of Israel, and the fulfillment of the promises made to Abraham. But Luke gives his history a much wider context by taking his genealogy all the way back to Adam. In doing so, Luke implies that the history of Jesus is the culmination not only of the history of Israel, but also of the entire history of humankind.

In summary, as a historian, Luke presents us with a narrative that is connected with the entire history of humanity as its continuation and culmination, but is also a new beginning in that history.

*   *   *

There is, however, another dimension of Luke's work as a historian that must be stressed: Luke tells us a story that does not end. It is unfinished both in its chronology and in its geography.

Let's take a closer look at this matter. Luke addresses his two books to Theophilus, a believer in Jesus Christ, and part of his purpose is to connect Theophilus with the life and teachings of Jesus by telling first about Jesus himself, and then about how his teachings spread through the land until they reached Theophilus and his contemporaries. In the second part of this history, Paul seems to become the main character to whom Luke devotes most of his narrative, telling us about his voyages, his evangelizing task, and finally his imprisonment and travel to Rome. But then he leaves us, so to speak, hanging in the air. As we finish reading the book of Acts, we immediately ask ourselves, *What happened to Paul?* But Luke doesn't say a word about this. After giving us all sorts of details about Paul's last voyage to Rome, and of the vicissitudes of the storm encountered and the eventual shipwreck, Luke leaves us wondering, simply telling us that Paul was preaching in Rome while he awaited his trial before Caesar.

This reminds me of the experience I had when I was about twelve years old and I read *The Narrative of Arthur Gordon Pym*, a novel by Edgar Allan Poe. The book was very interesting to a young man such as I, for it told of a series of maritime adventures, many of them hardly credible, but all of them fascinating. Like the story of Paul, the one about Pym included a shipwreck. Finally I reached the high point of the story, where Pym was facing a mysterious character who threatened his life. How would he come out of that encounter? But as I turned the page to find out, the story simply stopped. The ending that did not really end left me in the grips of an unquenchable curiosity. It was like those adventures of Tarzan that we heard on the radio every day at noon, ending always with cliffhangers like this: "Will Tarzan be able to rescue Jane from her enemies? Listen tomorrow for the outcome on this station, at this time." But the difference was that, in the case of Tarzan, my curiosity would be satisfied tomorrow, whereas in the case of Pym, it remains unsatisfied to this day, more than sixty years later.

Something similar happens with the book of Acts. It does not finish; it simply stops. It leaves us trying to find out what will happen next, what will happen to Paul. In other words, it is an unfinished story.

Furthermore, the story is unfinished not only in its chronology, but also in its geography. The story in two volumes that Luke tells us begins in Galilee, and throughout the Gospel moves between Galilee and Judea, between Nazareth and Jerusalem. From Nazareth in Galilee, Mary and Joseph go to Bethlehem in Judea, where Jesus is born. After a visit to the temple in Jerusalem to present the child, they return to Galilee. But every year they go to Jerusalem to celebrate the Passover. (Luke is the only Gospel writer who tells us about one of these visits when Jesus was twelve years old.) So, on the whole, the story moves from Galilee to Jerusalem. From chapter 4 to the end of chapter 9, Luke tells us about the ministry of Jesus in Galilee. Then, at the end of that chapter, in 9:51, he tells us that Jesus "set his face to go to Jerusalem." This begins an extensive section of this Gospel comprising Jesus' prolonged journey from Galilee to Jerusalem. The rest of the story takes place in Jerusalem, with two brief parentheses in Emmaus and in Bethany, both near Jerusalem itself.

But then, at the beginning of the second book, Luke offers us what may well be taken as a geographical outline for the rest of his story. Jesus says to his disciples, "You will be my witnesses in Jerusalem, in all Judea and Samaria, and to the ends of the earth" (Acts 1:8). As one reads the rest of the book, it becomes obvious that these words serve as a general outline of what will follow. The narrative begins in Jerusalem, where, as a result of the outpouring of the Spirit on Pentecost, the disciples become witnesses to the Lord. In chapter 8 we are told about Philip's ministry in Samaria. And the next chapter tells us about Peter's witness in some of the regions within Judea itself. In chapter 10, Peter goes to the Judean coast, where the conversion of Cornelius takes place. From that point on, the story moves to Antioch, and then from Antioch to Cyprus, Asia Minor, Macedonia, and finally Rome. All of this seems to be the fulfillment of the promise made in Acts 1:8, for the disciples are indeed witnesses in Jerusalem, in Judea, and in Samaria. But in fact the promise of Acts 1:8 is not fulfilled. Acts ends when Paul is in Rome, and Rome is far from being at "the ends of the earth"! On the contrary, many considered Rome the center of the earth. This is why one can say that Luke's story is unfinished, not only in terms of its chronology, but also in terms of its geography.

It is interesting to note that, precisely because the promise of Acts 1:8 is not fulfilled in Acts itself, soon Christians began developing stories and suppositions about how it was that the disciples did in fact become witnesses to the ends of the earth. Thus it was said that Thomas went to India, Philip to Byzantium, and James to Spain. In this last case, the legend about St. James was grounded on the geographical position of the Iberian Peninsula, at the end of the known world. It was thought without any doubt that the apostles had indeed preached throughout the entire earth, and this gave rise to the legend that James had gone to Spain, and even to Cape Finesterre, whose Latin name means "The End of the Earth."

But all these legends seem to undercut Luke's purpose, which is precisely to leave his story unfinished. A story with an ending interests us mostly for reasons of curiosity. Thus, for instance, we are interested in knowing about the lives of Augustus Caesar and Napoleon simply because they are important figures in history, because they help us understand the past. But whether or not Napoleon won the Battle of Austerlitz does not really touch us personally, nor does it require any action on our part. But an unfinished story is quite different. A story that gives us information but still goes on is an invitation: an invitation to join it, to continue it.

This is why Luke writes his history as he does: not only to inform us or to inform Theophilus, but also to invite both Theophilus and us to continue a history that is still ongoing — in a way, to live in chapter 29 of Acts, to contribute to the fulfillment of the promise that the disciples of the Lord will be witnesses "in Jerusalem, in Judea, in Samaria, and to the ends of the earth." So let us read Luke's two books as an invitation, and let us read his history as a guide and a call for the living of our own stories.

★   ★   ★

In what follows I make no attempt to systematize Luke's thought. Actually, I am convinced that any such systematization would tend to simplify and even to twist what Luke himself says. Luke is not writing or trying to write a systematic theology, or a book of doctrine, but rather a narrative about the life of Jesus and the life of the church. If one attempts to systematize such writings, what usually happens is that one excludes the narrative elements and leaves only the general and the abstract remaining. This in itself contradicts what the text itself says and tries to do.

What we can do is to follow Luke's narrative and note some of the points that he underscores, as well as some phrases which are indications of the way in which Luke writes his history. This will be our method in the pages that follow. Rather than posing abstract questions, we will focus our attention on the narrative itself and on how the manner in which Luke tells it illumines both his own history and his understanding of the gospel. Without further ado, let us turn to the first of such considerations, that of Luke as a historian, which in a way is an introduction to all that follows.

Luke and the History of Israel

Elizabeth was barren.
Luke 1:7

LUKE IS THE ONLY Gospel writer who tells us about the birth of John. Matthew, without further explication, tells us simply that "in those days John the Baptist appeared in the wilderness" (Matt. 3:1). Likewise, Mark says that "John the Baptizer appeared in the wilderness" (Mark 1:4). John is not much more explicit when he says simply that "there was a man sent by God, whose name was John" (John 1:6). In contrast to these three, Luke includes the announcement of the birth of John to his father, Zechariah; the announcement of the birth of Jesus to Mary; the visit of Mary to Elizabeth; the canticle of Zechariah; and several other details about John's birth and kindred. It is also important to note that in this entire narrative it is two women, Elizabeth and Mary, who stand at the center of the stage — a point to which we shall return when we deal with the matter of gender in Luke. For the present, we will center our attention on the story itself — the story of Elizabeth's barrenness and its relationship to Mary.

Luke is also the only one who tells us that "Elizabeth was barren." This assertion and the story that follows are not surprising to anyone who knows the history of Israel. That history begins with the barrenness of the elderly Sarah, which seemed to contradict the promise made to Abraham. But, through divine intervention,

Sarah conceives and gives birth to Isaac. Shortly thereafter, still in the book of Genesis, we are told that "Isaac prayed to the LORD for his wife, because she was barren; and the LORD granted his prayer, and his wife Rebekah conceived" (Gen. 25:21). The result is the birth of Esau and his twin brother, Jacob, who would later be known as Israel. Jacob marries first Leah and then her sister Rachel. Later on, in Genesis 29:31, we are told that Rachel too was barren until God took mercy on her and gave her two children, Joseph and Benjamin. And this theme of barrenness is not exhausted with the stories of the great matriarchs of Israel, but appears again in Judges, where the angel of the Lord tells Manoah's wife, "Although you are barren, having borne no children, you shall conceive and bear a son" (Judg. 13:3). This child is Samson, who defends Israel against the Philistines. Finally, one must remember the story of Hannah, who also was unable to conceive until God intervened in her life and gave her Samuel, whose very name, meaning "I asked God for him," is a reminder of his origin. In brief, in the history of Israel we repeatedly find the theme of a barren woman who conceives thanks to divine intervention, and whose child becomes a central figure in that history.

Luke now picks up the same subject, and at the very beginning of his Gospel tells us the story of Elizabeth and Zechariah. Once again, as in the stories of Sarah, Rebekah, Rachel, and Hannah, the barren woman will conceive, and her child will be a central figure in the history of the fulfillment of the promises made to Abraham centuries before. In this Gospel, John does not simply appear suddenly preaching, as in the other Gospels; he is the continuation of a long history which includes Isaac, Jacob, Joseph, Samson, and Samuel.

Luke moves on, and soon tells us that in Nazareth there was "a virgin engaged to a man whose name was Joseph, of the house of David" (Luke 1:27). Mary is a virgin, and therefore in a sense she is as barren as possible. In the former cases, the barren women asked God to be able to conceive, and God responded. In this case, it is

God who takes the initiative. Mary, without having known a man, will have a child. This child — like Isaac, Jacob, Joseph, Samson, and Samuel — will have an important place in God's plan. In a way, all those earlier births were announcements and signs pointing to this particular birth. But this birth is even more extraordinary than that of Isaac and the rest. It is a virgin birth. In this context, it is interesting to note that at one end and the other of this list of barren women are two acts of conception that are more marvelous than those of Rachel, Rebekah, and Hannah. At the beginning of the chain there is Sarah, an elderly woman, whose womb was dry. At the end, there is Mary, a young virgin.

⋆ ⋆ ⋆

This is an example of a manner of interpreting the history of Israel that was quite common in the ancient church, and is usually known as typology. Justin Martyr, an ancient Christian writer from a town near Antioch, where Luke seems to have lived, declared that in ancient times God spoke in two ways: by words and by actions. The former is usually called "prophecy," and does not need to detain us at present, for it is well-known. But speech through actions is something which we often forget, and which will take us back to the theme of the barren women. The premise of this sort of biblical interpretation is that God acts in certain patterns which resemble each other, and which point to their final fulfillment in Jesus Christ. These patterns are called "types," which is meaningfully similar to the word *typography*. It comes from two Greek roots, one meaning "type" and the other "writing." When we use the word *type* in this manner, we are referring to a certain pattern that appears repeatedly. Thus, for instance, the letters A and X may be written in different ways, but all the variants are recognizable as types of the same two letters. The word that interests us here, typology, is a combination of two roots, one meaning "type" and the other "reason," "logic," or "word." Thus, typological biblical interpretation sees the history of Israel as a series of "types" — that is, patterns which appear, although always in new and different ways, but all pointing to Jesus Christ.

A theme that appears repeatedly in the Bible, and that points to Jesus, is precisely the theme of the barren woman, which in the Gospel of Luke reappears in the person of Elizabeth and then comes to its culmination in Mary. Luke then reinforces that typology by relating Mary to Hannah, for the song of Mary in Luke (1:46-55) is parallel to the song of Hannah in 1 Samuel 2:1-10. Note, for instance, the parallelism between the two.

In Hannah's song we find these words:

Those who were full have hired themselves out for bread,
but those who were hungry are fat with spoil. (v. 5)

And in Mary's song we find these similar words:

He has filled the hungry with good things,
and sent the rich away empty. (v. 53)

We shall come back to these words later on, as we deal with the "great reversal" in Luke. But what interests us at present is that Mary, the virgin who conceives, is the culmination of a pattern that appears in Hannah, the barren woman who also conceives, and before her in Sarah, Rebekah, Rachel, and others. The son of Mary is the culmination of this history, which is also a history of Isaac, Jacob, Joseph, Samson, and Samuel.

★   ★   ★

However, the theme of the barren woman is not the only one in which Luke presents Jesus as the fulfillment of types of events that took place earlier in the history of Israel. By way of example, we may consider two others.

The first example of typology is the relationship between the redeeming action of God in Jesus and the redeeming action of God in leading Israel out of Egypt. For the Jewish people, that liberation from the yoke of Egypt revolved around the *pesah*, from which comes the Greek *pascha*, meaning "Passover." This was the day on which the angel of the Lord passed over the children of Israel, while destroying the firstborn of the Egyptians. In the book of Exodus, the angel knew the homes of the children of Israel because they had been marked with lamb's blood. Therefore, the price for the salvation of the firstborn of Israel was the blood of a lamb. Luke, as well as other authors in the New Testament and the ancient church, saw in this a type or sign of what would happen with Jesus, the Lamb sacrificed for the salvation of the people.

Luke adds another dimension to this. According to the law of Israel, every firstborn belonged by right to God, for the angel of the Lord had saved the firstborn in Egypt. In Numbers 3:13, God says, "All the firstborn are mine; when I killed all the firstborn in the land of Egypt, I consecrated for my own all the firstborn in Israel, both human and animal; they shall be mine. I am the LORD." For this reason, every firstborn had to be redeemed, rescued, or bought back by means of a sacrifice. This subject of the relationship of Jesus and the Law appears first of all in the story of the presentation at the temple, when Jesus' parents take him there in order to redeem him by sacrificing two birds. (It is interesting to note that in a sense, the Redeemer himself has to be redeemed, which is one more way in which Luke makes him fully human.) Thus, from the very beginning of his Gospel, Luke establishes a link between Jesus and the Passover and the liberation from Egypt.

This introduces a theme that will appear throughout the Third Gospel, as well as in much of ancient Christian literature: Jesus, freed from the law of Passover through his presentation at the temple, is also the Passover Lamb by whose blood believers are redeemed, just as the firstborn of Israel were redeemed from death, and the entire people were liberated from the yoke of Egypt. Luke, as well as Matthew and Mark, tells us that Jesus' last supper with his disciples before his crucifixion was a Passover meal. It was on that occasion that Jesus established the Lord's Supper, also called the Eucharist. But Luke adds a detail that does not appear in the other Gospels: Jesus and his family went to Jerusalem every year for the celebration of Passover. Every year Jesus partook of this meal, which was a type or figure of the Last Supper; and every year he ate of the lamb, which was a type of the manner in which he would redeem his people by his death.

The second example of typology is the very important relationship between Jesus and Adam. This relationship is stressed both by Luke and by Paul. If our writer was indeed a companion of Paul, he must have heard from him expressions such as those that appear in 1 Corinthians 15: "As all die in Adam, so all will be made alive in Christ. . . . Thus it is written, 'The first man, Adam, became a living being': the last Adam became a life-giving spirit" (vv. 22, 45). A similar idea appears in Romans 5:14, where Paul says that Adam "is a type of the one who was to come" — that is, Jesus.

Luke makes that connection between Adam and Jesus in his own ways too. His genealogy, besides including all humanity from its very beginnings, starts with Jesus. It begins immediately after Jesus' baptism, when God declares, "You are my son, the Beloved" (Luke 3:22). But then it ends with Adam, whom Luke calls "son of God" (Luke 3:38). At a certain level, this seems to say simply that Adam, in contrast with Enos, Seth, and all the rest, had no father other than God. But at a deeper level, this genealogy relates Adam, the beginning of the first creation and head of all humankind, to Jesus, the beginning of a new creation and head of a new humankind. It is interesting to note that Luke is the only one among the Four Evangelists who mentions Adam, and that this places him in a theological relationship with Paul, who among the writers of the New Testament is the one referring most frequently to Adam and the only one, besides Luke, who gives theological significance to Adam himself. This typology is present not only in this particular reference to Adam. It is also evident in (among other places) the temptation in the desert, an episode that appears in all three Synoptic Gospels. In Luke, this temptation appears immediately after the genealogy, which ends with "Adam, son of God." Now Jesus, the "son of God" in the strictest sense, is taken to the desert to be tempted — tempted in the desert as Adam was tempted in the garden, and therefore more sorely than Adam himself. In Genesis, Adam's temptation is seeking to be "like God"; he forgets that he has already been made in God's image and likeness, and that therefore he is already like God. In the desert, the devil tempts Jesus with the same doubt: "If you are the son of God. . . ." One may also point out that in the temptations of Jesus in the desert there are parallels with the temptation of Israel in the desert. For instance, the devil tempts Jesus to turn a stone into bread; earlier he tempted the children of Israel by making them think that God would not respond to their need for food. The type or pattern of Adam tempted in the garden appears again in the story of Israel tempted in the desert, and culminates in Jesus, tempted, like Israel, in the desert.

As we consider these typologies, it is clear that quite often Jesus is not only the culmination of but also the counterpoint to earlier times. Adam, tempted in the garden, succumbed. Israel, tempted in the desert, also succumbed. But Jesus, tempted in the desert, overcame the Evil One. Likewise, the sacrifice of the paschal lamb had to be repeated every year, while the sacrifice of

Jesus, the Lamb of God, took place once and for all and ended the need for expiatory sacrifices.

*   *   *

It is also important to point out that, while the various types in the Old Testament find their fulfillment in Jesus, this does not mean an end to typology. On the contrary: the patterns that appear repeatedly in the history of Israel, leading to their culmination in Jesus, continue to appear again and again in the history of the church. Thus, in Galatians 4, Paul takes the pattern of the barren woman appearing in Sarah in order to transfer it to the New Jerusalem, "the mother of us all" — that is, the church or the fellowship of believers, joyfully applying to it the words of Isaiah: "Sing, O barren one who did not bear" (Isa. 54:1). In the case of Luke, this becomes clear in the book of Acts. The very story of Pentecost has typological dimensions. Part of what Israel celebrated on that date was the gift of the Law of Moses, and therefore the birth of Israel as a people. Now on this new Pentecost comes the gift of the Spirit, and thereby the creation of the church as a people. At Sinai, the tribes of Israel became a people thanks to the gift of the Law. Now, on Pentecost, Parthians, Medes, Elamites, and many others come to be a people thanks to the gift of the Spirit. In Acts 7, the death of Stephen also has typological dimensions, for his trial reminds us of the trial of Jesus, and his words at the moment of death echo those of Jesus from the cross. And the same may be said about the miracles and sufferings of the apostles, which also reflect the miracles and sufferings of Jesus.

Therefore, typology is not only a matter of an ancient history coming to its culmination in Jesus; it is also a matter of the present, where we find circumstances similar to those that the people of God had to face in earlier times, and present-day believers have the opportunity to show that they are part of that story. In Luke 20:17, Jesus refers to himself by interpreting typologically what Psalm 118:22 says about "the stone that the builders rejected." The same theme appears in Peter's speech in Acts 4:11. But the theme of the rejected stone that has become a cornerstone, which applies primarily to Jesus, also applies to the disciples throughout the writings of Luke. And, just as the same Jesus who was rejected has become the cornerstone, so his disciples — persecuted, besieged, flogged, and imprisoned — will be vindicated. (This image immediately reminds us of First Peter, where believers are compared to stones in the house or temple that God is building.)

All of this may seem very strange to us in the twenty-first century. How is it that one can say that, without repeating itself, history follows certain patterns, and that those patterns help us understand the history of Israel, the history of Jesus, and our own history? Could this be a strange notion that occurred to an overly imaginative mind in ancient times? Quite clearly, most of the people around us do not speak in this manner!

On this point, it is important to say first of all that typology is a constant characteristic in the biblical record. One may take as an example the story of Exodus. When, centuries later, Israel finds itself once again captive, although now in Babylon, the prophet rejoices at the promise of a return from exile, and does this in terms that are parallel to the story of the Exodus and to the psalms that celebrated it. Naturally, there are differences, for Babylon is not Egypt, and the desert is not the Red Sea. But this use of typology can easily be seen by looking, for instance, at Isaiah 43, in which the crossing of the Red Sea becomes a prototype for the return from exile:

Thus says the LORD,
who makes a way in the sea,

> *a path in the mighty waters,*
> *who brings out chariot and horse,*
> *army and warrior;*
> *they lie down, they cannot rise,*
> *they are extinguished,*
> *quenched like a wick:*
> *Do not remember the former things,*
> *or consider the things of old.*
> *I am about to do a new thing;*
> *now it springs forth,*
> *do you not perceive it?*
> *I will make a way in the wilderness*
> *and rivers in the desert.* (Isa. 43:16-19)

Note that here, at the same time that the redeeming action of God is remembered, the purpose is not to remain in the past, not to remember that past with mere longing, but rather to see in those past actions of God promises of a new action, for once again God will open the way out of captivity.

But the return from exile is not the end of the Exodus typology. When Mark, the earliest Evangelist, tells the story of Jesus, he begins by referring to John the Baptist as a "voice crying out in the wilderness" (Mark 1:3), and then Matthew and Luke, following Mark, use exactly the same words (Matt. 3:3; Luke 3:4). When we hear these words, we usually interpret them to mean that no one will heed the Baptist's cries. It is thus that we often refer to someone as a "voice crying out in the wilderness," meaning that, even though what this particular person says is true, nobody listens. But this is not what the Evangelists mean by that phrase. What they are doing is linking John with Isaiah. For just as in the desert Isaiah announced the great liberation of the people from exile, so now another voice in the wilderness, John, announces the liberation that Jesus is to bring. Thus develops another typological chain, leading from the Exodus to the Exile, and from the Exile to Jesus. And then Luke continues that chain with the story of the Transfiguration, when he tells us that Moses and Elijah were speaking with Jesus about "his departure." The word that the NRSV translates as "departure," which does not appear in the story as Matthew tells it, is "exodus." Thus, the death, resurrection, and ascension of Jesus will be like a new Exodus in which the people have to suffer oppression and pain before being liberated, and, as in the Exile, suffering will come before restoration.

It is important for us to recognize that it is not only Luke who interprets the scriptures of Israel and its history typologically. On the contrary, this sort of interpretation appears throughout Scripture, and the reason for clarifying it is that it helps us understand not only Luke but also the other biblical authors.

⋆   ⋆   ⋆

And when we stop to think about it, we realize that it is not only in biblical interpretation and in a religious and theological context that we employ typology. In a way, we live our entire lives on the basis of typological interpretations of reality. Let's consider the earlier example of the sun, which rises every morning. Every dawn is different from the ones that preceded it — but dawn always comes. That's why we count on a new dawn tomorrow — because we have seen a pattern for the sun's rising. The pattern is the same, but each of its manifestations is different. And other patterns repeat themselves as well. So there is the ongoing importance of repeated patterns in our lives.

Another example that applies directly to those of us who are preachers or frequent public speakers is that as we prepare, we do not know how many people will be present, who they will be, what the weather will be like, and other such details. Therefore, we have to prepare in almost total ignorance of what will happen when we speak. But notice that I said "almost total ignorance" — because on many other occasions we have found ourselves in similar situations, because we have heard friends and colleagues preach and speak, because we know that the audience, although certainly not exactly the same as on other occasions, will have similar interests. Thus, in preparing for a sermon or a speech, we must rely on past patterns — patterns whose repetition we expect, but which will not appear in exactly the same manner as they did before. What all of this means is that when Luke and the other biblical authors make use of typology, they are simply doing what all of us do in our daily lives.

But there is a critical difference: in daily life, although there are ups and downs, there is no overwhelming culmination, no final point that defines everything and toward which everything marches. Many, especially in past times when there was a particular sort of religious fervor, turned death into that point of culmination. This suggested that humans live in order to die, that all of life's meaning is in death. Thus, there were monks who every day would dig a bit of their own graves as a daily reminder that life leads to death. Today, many of us live in expectation of another high point in life: when I graduate, when I marry, when I have children, when my grandchildren go to school. We all seek an anchor, a crucial point that will give meaning to life.

But in Christian typology, there is indeed a high point. This high point is none other than Jesus Christ. All the biblical stories point to him, from Genesis, through Exodus, through the Exile, through the words and actions of the prophets, up to John the Baptist. And if we take seriously the fact that Luke draws his genealogy all the way back to Adam, one might dare suggest that were we to ask Luke, he would tell us that Jesus is not only the culmination of the history of Israel, but the high point of all human history. There-fore, all those names that Luke gives of rulers and great figures in the world of the Gentiles — Augustus Caesar, Tiberius, Quirin-ius, Sergius Paulus, Porcius Festus, and the rest — are not only a way of dating events, but also a reminder that the history of Israel takes place within the context of the history of all humanity, and that Jesus Christ, the high point in the history of Israel, is also the culmination of all human history.

This gives the book of Acts a dimension that we often forget. Acts is not only the history of the expansion of Christianity through the work of Paul and others; it is also the beginning of the process through which Jesus Christ announces and claims his lordship over all history and all humankind. But it is necessary to be clear on one point: this is the lordship of Jesus Christ, not the lordship of Christians or even of Christianity. When these two are confused, we fall into the trap of missionary colonialism, in which mission is confused with imposing our way of thinking and doing things on others. What is taking place in Acts is not only that the disciples are taking their faith to new places, but also that in those new places the disciples discover that the action of God was present even be-fore they got there. This may be seen, for instance, in Acts 10, in the episode of Cornelius and Peter, and then in chapter 11, where, thanks to the witness of Cornelius, the entire church discovers new horizons for its mission.

Thus, typology is important for two reasons: first, because it underscores that this is the way in which the past helps us to un-derstand Jesus Christ and his work; and, second, because this is the manner in which Jesus Christ and his work lead us to see the past, the present, and the future.

At the beginning of Acts, immediately after the Ascension, the disciples receive their promise: "This Jesus, who has been taken up from you into heaven, will come in the same way as you saw him go into heaven" (Acts 1:11). In other words, this Jesus Christ who is the culmination of all the events that announced him is also the pattern unlocking all the events which are to follow, particularly in the lives of those who await Christ's return. (Let's take another example from 1 Peter: there we see that the stone that the builders rejected is a type of Jesus, but that those who believe in him are like stones who are to join the temple of God, and that they too are to suffer as rejected stones.)

In Luke, the typology that helps us understand Jesus in the light of the history of Israel and of humanity is also the typology that helps us understand our own lives and our own stories in the light of Jesus. According to that typology, the stone that was rejected has become the cornerstone. According to the same typology, those who today are despised are the ones for whom the crown of victory is reserved. This is in essence the next basic theme in Luke's theology, "the great reversal," which we will discuss in the next chapter.

THREE

Luke and the Great Reversal

He has brought down the powerful from their thrones.

Luke 1:52

O NE OF THE CENTRAL themes in the Gospel of Luke is what interpreters have often called "the great reversal" — or perhaps in today's more common language we should call it "the world upside down." This theme appears in the very beginning of the Gospel, in the song of Mary that is usually known by the first word of its Latin translation, *Magnificat*. The canticle begins this way: *Magnificat anima mea Dominum* — "My soul magnifies the Lord." But in truth the theme is not just the praise of God, but rather the praise of the God who is the Lord of great upheavals. Mary praises God because "he has looked with favor on the lowliness of his servant" and because God "has done great things for me." And then she places her own exaltation in the context of a great upheaval:

> *He has shown strength with his arm;*
> *he has scattered the proud in the thoughts of their hearts.*
> *He has brought down the powerful from their thrones,*
> *and lifted up the lowly;*
> *he has filled the hungry with good things,*
> *and sent the rich away empty.*
> *He has helped his servant Israel,*
> *in remembrance of his mercy.* . . . *(Luke 1:51-54)*

As noted before, this hymn echoes Hannah's canticle in 1 Samuel. There we find the following lines:

> My heart exults in the LORD;
>   my strength is exalted in my God.
> My mouth derides my enemies,
>   because I rejoice in my victory.
>
> . . .
>
> The bows of the mighty are broken,
>   but the feeble gird on strength.
> Those who were full have hired themselves out for bread,
>   but those who were hungry are fat with spoil.
> The barren has borne seven,
>   but she who has many children is forlorn.
>
> . . .
>
> The LORD makes poor and makes rich;
>   he brings low, he also exalts.
> He raises up the poor from the dust;
>   he lifts the needy from the ash heap,
> to make them sit with princes
>   and inherit a seat of honor. (1 Sam. 2:1, 4-5, 7-8)

In her song, Hannah praises God for the great reversal that is taking place in her life. The book of Samuel begins by telling us about Elkanah and his two wives, Hannah and Peninnah. Although Elkanah loved Hannah, Peninnah tormented her, for she had children and Hannah did not. Because that society prized fertility and child-bearing, Hannah was ashamed of her barrenness, and apparently her rival used this as an opportunity to goad and sadden her. The rest of the story is well-known. Hannah's prayers are answered, and finally the barren conceives.

In that context, Hannah praises God because, as she says, "My strength is exalted in my God. My mouth derides my enemies." Hannah rejoices over what God has done in her, and from that point moves to a series of affirmations about how this action is a pattern for God's other actions — which leads us back to the theme of typology and the patterns of divine action. Thus, Hannah sings not only because God has allowed her to conceive, but also because the God who has so blessed her is also the God who breaks the bows of the strong and gives strength to the weak; the God who makes the rich have to rent themselves out for bread, and gives food to the hungry.

Note that both the song of Hannah and the song of Mary begin with the exaltation of the one who sings, but then move on to a more general praise of the God who not only does mighty things, but also turns the world upside down, exalting the humble and bringing down the mighty from their thrones, feeding the hungry and making those who are overfed work for their bread, breaking the bows of the strong and giving strength to the weak. In other words, both women praise God for the great reversal that the divine intervention brings about, not only in their lives, but in society in general.

This great reversal that Luke introduces in the song of Mary appears throughout his writings, in both the Gospel and Acts. It would be a mistake to think that Luke is the only one who develops this theme, because it appears quite frequently in the Bible, and certainly is found in some of the parallel texts in Matthew and Mark. Furthermore, the explicit phrase "some are last who will be first, and some are first who will be last" (Luke 13:30), which appears only once in Luke, appears repeatedly in both Matthew and Mark. (See, for instance, Matt. 19:30; 20:16; 20:17; Mark 9:35; 10:31; 10:44.) But even though Luke employs that phrase only once, the theme to which that phrase points appears repeatedly and pointedly both in his Gospel and in Acts.

*   *   *

This great reversal is both religious and social. Even though such distinctions were not made then as they are now, it may be profitable for us to discuss them in order.

The great religious upheaval appears early in the Gospel of Luke. In chapter 4, Luke tells us about the preaching of Jesus in a synagogue in his own land. Both Matthew and Mark say simply that Jesus taught in the synagogue, and that people marveled that Jesus, whom they all knew as a carpenter's son, was able to teach in this manner. Apparently because of that familiarity, they disbelieved, and for this reason, Jesus did not perform many miracles in their midst. Related to this, in Matthew as well as in Mark, is Jesus' comment that "prophets are not without honor except in their country and in their own house" (Matt. 13:57; Mark 6:14).

Luke gives more details. He tells us first of all that the text that Jesus read was taken from the prophet Isaiah, and he also tells us what it was that Jesus preached. The comment about a prophet not being honored in his own land does not appear at the end of the narrative, as in the other two Synoptic Gospels, but rather at the beginning, as an introduction to Jesus' sermon. The sermon itself then becomes an illustration or explanation of this saying. Jesus tells his neighbors that in the time of the prophet Elijah, when there was a great famine, there were many needy widows in Israel. Yet Elijah did not go to any of them, but rather to a widow of Zarephath in Sidon — that is, a Gentile widow living in a city-state known for its enmity to Israel. And in the time of the next prophet, Elisha, there were many lepers in Israel, but Elisha did not heal any of them; instead, he healed Naaman, who was from Syria, the great enemy of Israel. Indeed, Jesus made a point of saying that these two great prophets did not show favor toward the widows or lepers of Israel, but rather toward a Phoenician widow and a Syrian general.

When Jesus said this, "all in the synagogue were filled with rage" and sought to kill him. It is important to note that the people's rage was not triggered, as we often think, by Jesus' daring to claim that "today this scripture has been fulfilled in your hearing." On the contrary, even after Jesus said those words, Luke tells us, "All spoke well of him and were amazed at the gracious words that came from his mouth" (Luke 4:22). The wrath of the congregation was aroused because Jesus told them through his stories about the prophets that, even though they were his neighbors, and even though they were children of Israel, this should not lead them to expect privileges from God.

Later on, in chapter 6, Luke tells us that those who came to listen to Jesus and to be healed by him came not only from all of Judea, but also "from the coast of Tyre and Sidon" (Luke 6:17). In chapter 7 — in a passage that has a parallel in Matthew but not in Mark — Jesus says about a Roman centurion who is a pagan, "not even in Israel have I found such faith" (Luke 7:9). In other words, when it comes to faith, this pagan has an advantage over even the most religious people in Israel. Shortly thereafter, Luke places in the mouth of Jesus words that do not appear in the other Gospels. Commenting on John the Baptist, Luke tells us that the common people heeded his words and even the tax collectors were baptized — that is, the most despised people in Israel, most despised because they not only were agents of the foreign invader, but also were in constant touch with the unclean and because they handled idolatrous coins. In contrast, we are told that "the Pharisees and the lawyers rejected God's purposes for themselves" (Luke 7:30). And, still in chapter 7, Jesus defends the worth of a sinful woman to a Pharisee who has invited him to dinner.

In chapter 14, in a passage that has no parallel in the other Gospels, Jesus tells a parable about a man who prepared a great feast, but when the time came for the special meal, all his invitees offered excuses. At that point the man ordered his slave to go out into the streets and lanes of the town and invite any person in need to the great dinner. This included particularly "the poor, the crippled, the blind, and the lame" (Luke 14:21) — that is, people who were often considered sinners and thought of as cursed by their sin. None of the religious people — those who were first given the invitation — enjoyed the banquet, while the guests of the last minute did. Since the parable begins with an allusion to the great banquet in the reign of God, it is clear that Jesus is telling those who boast that they were first to receive the word of God must not presume that for that reason they will enjoy the final banquet.

Very soon after that parable, in chapter 15, there is the parable of the lost sheep, which does have a parallel in Matthew 18. This is a well-known parable, for it gives us hope and consolation when we are like the lost sheep. But in Luke the parable is more biting, for Jesus is actually reprimanding the Pharisees and the scribes — the leaders in religious matters — who criticize him for eating with publicans and sinners. Within that context, what stands out is not only the value of the lost sheep, but also the point, seldom noticed today, that the shepherd leaves the ninety-nine in the wilderness. In a great reversal, the lost sheep is cared for while the ninety-nine who are already with the shepherd are simply left on their own.

Something similar may be said about the well-known parable of the prodigal son, which appears only in the Gospel of Luke. Once again, we imagine that the main character is the prodigal, and that the theme of the parable is the love of the father who receives the wayward son. But the parable does not end with the return of the prodigal, for there is another character who is equally important: his older brother. He has served his father faithfully in his brother's absence, obeying him in all things. And now that his younger brother returns and is received with a feast, he refuses to go in, because he is better than the one who has just returned from distant lands. Another great reversal!

After another series of parables — among them the one about the rich man and Lazarus, to which we shall return — the entire theme of the great reversal comes to a high point in the parable of the Pharisee and the tax collector, in which the tax collector who confesses his sin is deemed more sincere than the Pharisee who declares himself religious, and Jesus ends by saying that "all who exalt themselves will be humbled, but all who humble themselves will be exalted" (Luke 18:14).

This great reversal that is central to the Gospel of Luke appears also in Acts, where the pagan Cornelius has a clearer vision than the apostle Peter, where the "Pharisee of Pharisees" who goes to Damascus in order to persecute the disciples of the Lord becomes one of the most faithful among those disciples, and where Paul and Barnabas repeatedly come face to face with the unbelief of those who should have believed (for they had the scriptures), contrasting with the openness of the Gentiles to the gospel.

*   *   *

This great religious reversal also has social dimensions. This appears most clearly in the parable of the rich man and Lazarus. Lazarus "longed to satisfy his hunger with what fell from the rich man's table" (Luke 16:21). But after both men die, Lazarus is in heaven by Abraham's side, and the rich man is in Hades. So in the end it is the rich man who begs Abraham to send Lazarus to "dip the tip of his finger and cool my tongue" (Luke 16:24). The reversal takes place between the rich and the poor, between the poor one who would have been satisfied with scraps and the wealthy one who now begs for water.

The theme of the poor and their place in the kingdom appears in the Third Gospel much more often than in any of the others. The word *poor* or *needy* appears only five times in Matthew, and the same number of times in Mark. Two of those references occur in the context of the suggestion that the alabaster jar — filled with the precious ointment that Mary poured on Jesus' head — should have been sold in order to give the proceeds to the poor. In contrast, Luke is constantly speaking about the poor and the needy.

This can be seen at the very beginning of Jesus' public ministry, in the text he reads in the synagogue: "The Spirit of the Lord is upon me, because he has anointed me to bring good news to the poor" (Luke 4:18). This particular passage is important, because as we analyze the structure of Luke's writings, we note that in both the Gospel and Acts there is a text from the Old Testament that is quoted near the beginning of the book and that outlines an important theme that is to follow. In Acts, it is the text from Joel that Peter quotes on the day of Pentecost. In Luke, it is the passage from Isaiah that serves to frame the rest of the book. And in this passage the very first thing that is said about the mission of Jesus is that he has been sent to bring "good news to the poor." (However, one must not exaggerate the contrast among the Gospels on this particular point. Both in Matthew [11:5] and in Luke [7:23], when the disciples of John ask Jesus if he is the one who has been expected, among the signs that Jesus gives them is the fact that "the gospel is announced to the poor.")

The Beatitudes are one of the many places where we see Luke's emphasis on poverty and on the great reversal the believers are to expect. Many of us know by heart the First Beatitude according to Matthew: "Blessed are the poor in spirit, for theirs is the kingdom of heaven" (Matt. 5:3). Although this probably does not mean a spiritual poverty in contrast to material riches, it certainly is possible to understand it as such. But Luke leaves no doubt about meaning when he says, "Blessed are you who are poor, for yours is the kingdom of God" (Luke 6:20). Here there is no place for a "spiritual" poverty in contrast to a material one. It is also interesting to note that while Matthew's beatitude refers to "the poor" in the third person, as if they were not present, Luke's beatitude directly addresses the poor: "Blessed are *you* who are poor." And to make matters clearer, Luke includes a series of woes that are the counterpart of the Beatitudes. In the case of the poor, the counterpart is "But woe to you who are rich, for you have received your consolation" (Luke 6:24). Furthermore, most of the Beatitudes in Luke have to do with the social and material conditions in which people live: "Blessed are you who are poor, . . . you who are hungry now, . . . you who weep now. . . ." And the reversal is underscored in the woes: "You who are rich, . . . you who are full now, . . . you who are laughing now. . . ."

The great reversal in the Gospel of Luke between the rich and the poor comes to a climax when Jesus, while a guest at the home of a Pharisee leader, dares to criticize his host's guest list:

> When you give a luncheon or a dinner, do not invite your friends
> or your brothers or your relatives or rich neighbors, in case they
> may invite you in return, and you would be repaid. But when
> you give a banquet, invite the poor, the crippled, the lame, and
> the blind. And you will be blessed, because they cannot repay
> you, for you will be repaid at the resurrection of the righteous.
> (Luke 14:12-15)

Having noted this emphasis of the Gospel of Luke on the poor and the needy, we may at first be surprised that the theme does not appear in Acts beyond chapter 4, where Luke tells us that among the disciples of the Lord, no one was needy. But this should not surprise us if we remember what the presence of the needy implies among the people of God. In order to understand this, we may turn our attention to a passage that appears in Matthew and Mark, but not in Luke. It is these famous words of Jesus: "For you always have the poor with you" (Matt. 26:11; Mark 14:7). To this day, these words are often used in order to avoid paying too much attention to the needs of the poor. But in these passages Jesus is actually quoting Deuteronomy 15:11, where, amid the regulations concerning the Year of Jubilee, when all property is to be restored to its former owners, the law commands that this regulation not be used as an excuse not to help the needy in the interim. As the people await the Jubilee, they must be liberal in their support of the needy.

Almost at the beginning of the Gospel, Luke tells us that in his first sermon Jesus declared that in him the promise of Isaiah was fulfilled, and part of his mission was "to proclaim the year of the Lord's favor" — that is, the Year of Jubilee. It is as a result of that preaching by Jesus, and of the gift of the Spirit in Acts, that the church is born. And Luke then tells us that, since the church lived in a constant jubilee, "there was not a needy person among them, for as many as owned lands or houses sold them and brought the proceeds of what was sold. They laid it at the apostles' feet, and it was distributed to each as any had need" (Acts 4:34-35). This is why, after this chapter, Luke no longer speaks of the needy. (However, we do know from the epistles of Paul that when there was a need in Jerusalem, the churches in other cities contributed to an offering for the poor in Jerusalem.) Apparently, Luke does not quote Jesus' saying "For you always have the poor with you" because his vision of an ideal church is of a people of God that lives in a constant jubilee, and in which therefore there are no poor.

In summary, the theme of the great reversal, which is seen in religious terms in what Jesus says to the scribes, Pharisees, tax collectors, and sinners, may be seen also in economic and social terms in what he says about the poor and the rich, and in the result of the presence of the Spirit in the church, thanks to which there are no longer any needy.

The great reversal also takes place in other dimensions of social life. One of them is the matter of gender, which deserves particular attention in our study, and therefore will be reserved for the next chapter. Another of the social dimensions of the great reversal has to do with the ethnic and cultural divisions of the time. Once again, it is important to remember that the distinction that we make today between such matters and religious issues did not exist in antiquity, and therefore prejudice and ethnic and racial divisions were based on religious matters.

Were we to draw a series of concentric circles, with Jerusalem and Judea at the center, we would see that the next circle of prejudice and exclusion was that of the Galileans. Galileans were Jews, but they did not live in Judea, for Samaria stood between Galilee and Judea. Also, Greeks, Romans, and other neighboring peoples had left their mark on Galilee, to the point that already in the time of Isaiah it was called "Galilee of the Gentiles" (Isa. 9:1, quoted also in Matt. 4:15). For the same reason, John tells us that Nathaniel asks, "Can anything good come out of Nazareth?" (John 1:46). And later in the same Gospel the Pharisees declare that no prophet has ever come out of Galilee (John 7:52). The Judean Jews — those from Judea — spoke the Aramaic of the region, and so did the Galileans. But the Judeans believed that the Galilean accent was inferior.

A bit further out from the center than the Galileans were the Hellenistic Jews, those in the Diaspora or Dispersion, who lived in distant lands and whose most common language was not Aramaic, but most often Greek. Hellenistic Jews were considered inferior by Jews in Palestine because they lived among pagans by whom they inevitably would be contaminated, and they did not attend the temple as frequently as the Judeans. For a long time after the conquests of Alexander, the Jews had struggled to keep their cultural and religious purity in the face of Hellenistic influx. Therefore, the Jews of the Diaspora, often called "Hellenists" or even "Greeks," were not well regarded by the more conservative Jews in the Holy Land.

If we then continue with our series of concentric circles, we shall see that beyond the Galileans and the Hellenistic Jews were the Samaritans. Due to a complicated series of historical circum-stances, the inhabitants of Samaria, who claimed to be descendants of Israel, followed a different version of the faith of Israel than that of the Jews. Their Pentateuch differed in some points from the Jewish Pentateuch, and they insisted that the proper place for God's temple was Mount Gerizim. For all these reasons, Jews, including Judeans as well as Galileans and even Hellenists, looked down on them and considered them infidels. This is the background of the parable of the Good Samaritan in Luke as well as of the story of the woman by the well in John 4.

In the next concentric circle were those whom Jews called "God-fearers," who were Gentiles who believed in the God and the moral laws of Israel and sought to live according to them, but for some reason did not formally convert to Judaism. In the Lukan literature there are several examples and references to such people — for instance, the Ethiopian eunuch and Cornelius the centurion.

Finally, still further out were the pagans, who did not believe in the true God. Most of them were idolaters and polytheists. They were contaminated by eating all sorts of unclean animals and by practicing various sorts of impurity and impiety. What's more, since the Romans were among these Gentiles, the Jewish nation saw in them the invading enemy, the extortionist power that imposed onerous taxes, the pagans who dared bring their idolatrous eagles to Jerusalem itself, and the power of occupation that had grown in Caesarea, a city that was markedly Roman and pagan — and not too far from Jerusalem.

The great reversal in Luke affects each of these categories. To begin with, although Jesus is born in Bethlehem of Judea, his family is from Galilee, and he is raised in Galilee. It is there that he begins his public ministry, and it is from that area that he draws his closest disciples. When looked at from this perspective, the story of the long journey to Jerusalem that occupies a central portion in the Gospel of Luke but not in the other Gospels is a story in which the periphery marches toward the center, and the center resists to the point of crucifying Jesus. In Luke 13, some ask Jesus about certain Galileans whom Pilate had ordered killed, and Jesus comments that these Galileans were no worse sinners than the eighteen Judeans on whom the tower of Siloam had fallen. In the final instance, the entire process of the trial and crucifixion of Jesus includes a strong element of resistance on the part of the Judeans against this Galilean band and their leader, who seemed to have taken the city and the temple by storm.

As for the Samaritans, the prejudice against them on the part of the Jews may be seen in Luke 9:52-53, when Jesus begins his final journey to Jerusalem. Since he has to go through Samaria, he sends messengers to prepare a place for him in a Samaritan village. But the villagers will not receive the messengers, for they know that Jesus is going to Jerusalem. Significantly, when the disciples want to have fire fall upon the village, Jesus tells them that he has not come to destroy souls, but to save them — which implies that his mission is also to the Samaritans.

Then, in chapter 10, in another of the parables that appear only in Luke, when a traveler who may be presumed to be a Jew lies wounded by the roadside, and two of the Jewish religious leaders do not help him, it is a Samaritan who stops and takes care of him. And let us not forget that this occurs on the road from Jerusalem to Jericho — that is, in Judea — and therefore the Samaritan himself is a foreigner who has to take into account the reigning prejudices against him.

A bit later, in chapter 17, when Jesus goes into a village between Galilee and Samaria, ten lepers come to him, and Jesus sends them to the priests, who are the ones who according to the law can declare them to be clean. On the way they are all healed, but only one of them comes back to thank Jesus, and this one is a Samaritan. On this occasion, Jesus comments, "Was none of them found to return and give praise to God except this foreigner?" (Luke 17:18).

*   *   *

If we then turn to the tensions between Palestinian Jews and those from the Diaspora — that is, Hellenistic Jews — we find an interesting reversal in chapter 6 of Acts, where we find the story of the distribution to the widows. The Hellenists complain that their widows are not being treated as well as the others. The response of the church is to elect a group of seven who are to be in charge of the distribution to all the widows, both those from Judea and those who are Hellenists. Specifically, the church elects Stephen, Philip, Prochorus, Nicanor, Timon, Parmenas, and Nicolaus. Note that all of these have names of Greek origin, and therefore they probably were part of the marginalized group of Hellenists. Furthermore, one of them, Nicolaus, was not even a Jew by birth, for Luke tells us that he was "a proselyte from Antioch" (Acts 6:5). In a significant part of the rest of the story in Acts, Paul and Barnabas together address their mission primarily to the Hellenistic Jews, for wherever they arrive, they begin by preaching at the synagogue. (Paul subsequently continues this mission on his own.)

But the Lukan material is not content with attacking prejudice against Galileans, Samaritans, and Hellenistic Jews, for it also opens the way for Gentiles. As early as Luke 13, we see Jesus telling a group of Jews that on the final day, when Abraham, Isaac, and the rest of the ancient leaders of Israel will be present, this group will be excluded. And in verses 29-30, immediately after this dire warning, Jesus adds, "Then people will come from east and west, from north and south, and will eat in the kingdom of God. Indeed, some are last who will be first, and some are first who will be last." And this word of Jesus begins to be fulfilled in the narrative of Acts, in which it becomes clear that the Gentiles are progressively and rapidly joining the people of God. Quite a reversal — both religious and ethnic!

The great reversal is closely related to what was said previously about biblical typology, in which certain patterns in God's action appear repeatedly, although always in a different way, until they reach their high point — Jesus, who is the fundamental pattern or archetype of all history. In Luke 20:17, Jesus applies to himself the words of Psalm 118: "The stone that the builders rejected has become the cornerstone." Similar words are found also in Matthew (21:42) and in Mark (12:10). In Acts 4, when Peter appears before the council of the Jews, he makes a similar declaration: "This Jesus is the stone that was rejected by you, the builders; it has become the cornerstone" (v. 11). And the same notion appears in 1 Peter, once again referring to Jesus (2:6-7). But the great reversal must also be seen in the life of the church, and in the reign of God that this life foreshadows. This is why, almost at the end of his Gospel, Luke tells us of a dispute among the disciples about who among them will be the greatest, and Jesus answers:

> The kings of the Gentiles lord it over them; and those in authority over them are called benefactors. But not so with you; rather the greatest among you must become like the youngest, and the leader like one who serves. (Luke 22:25-26)

For Luke, as for all believers, the resurrection, ascension, and final triumph of Jesus comprise the axis around which all history revolves. But the Resurrection is not a culmination of a life of glory, power, and honors; rather, it comes after a life of constant persecution culminating in the insults during his trial in the praetorium and on the cross of Calvary. Luke's Jesus is, in the words of Isaiah, "a man of suffering and acquainted with infirmity." But he is also the conqueror of the grave and death. The story that begins in the remote and forgotten village of Nazareth will eventually lead to Rome, and even that is not its culmination.

At the beginning of the Gospel, Luke tells us how, in the time of Augustus Caesar, Jesus was born in a manger because there was no place for him in the inn. Towards the end of his narrative, in Acts 17, Luke tells us that Paul and his companions were accused of subverting the decrees of Caesar by "saying that there is another king named Jesus" (Acts 17:7). The story that begins in the manger also tells us that Stephen saw the glory of God and Jesus seated at the right hand of God (Acts 7:54-56). From the manger outside the inn to the right hand of God — that is the great reversal which is at the very foundation of all the other reversals to which Luke refers!

FOUR

Luke and Gender

There was also a prophet, Anna.

Luke 2:36

ONE OF THE MOST important contributions of the last decades to biblical interpretation has been the rediscovery of matters of gender as a hermeneutical key, at least for certain texts. As we look at Luke's writings — the Third Gospel as well as Acts — we find that among all the writers of the New Testament, it is Luke who includes the most frequent references to women and their place in the history of salvation. This occurs so often, in fact, that in discussions of who the author of these two books might be, there are some who suggest that the author is a woman who came to be known as "Luke." This "new naming" was done to prevent the diminishment of the credibility of her two books at a time toward the end of the first century and the beginning of the second, when the authority and the role of women in the church were being increasingly restricted.

But even apart from such suggestions and the debates that may arise from them, there is no doubt that among all the writings of the New Testament, the Third Gospel and Acts pay the most attention to women. Even a rapid reading of the biblical text will soon show this.

★   ★   ★

The story of the birth of Jesus appears only in the Gospels of Matthew and Luke. We are so used to reading these two stories as if they were a single one that we don't notice that Matthew focuses more on Joseph than on Mary. In that Gospel, we are told that Mary was betrothed to Joseph and that "she was found to be with child from the Holy Spirit" (Matt. 1:18). But then the attention turns to Joseph and his reaction on learning that Mary is pregnant. We are not told a word about how Mary reacted. Furthermore, when we come to the birth itself, Mary is not even mentioned: Matthew simply says that "Jesus was born in Bethlehem of Judea" (Matt. 2:1), without giving further news about his mother. In fact, Matthew doesn't mention Mary again until the wise men come from the east to see Jesus: "On entering the house, they saw the child with Mary, his mother" (2:11). Then comes the story of the flight to Egypt, in which the central character is Joseph. After the angel gave him instructions, he "got up, took the child and his mother by night, and went to Egypt, and remained there until the death of Herod" (Matt. 2:14-15). Note that in this entire sentence the subject is Joseph.

In sharp contrast is Luke's narrative of the birth, in which women have a central place. It is true that at the beginning of the Gospel one hears mostly about Zechariah. We are told that he was married to Elizabeth and that "*both of them* were righteous before God, living blamelessly according to all the commandments and regulations of the Lord" (Luke 1:6; my italics). This is followed by Zechariah's vision, in which he is told that Elizabeth, who until then had been barren, will conceive. At this point the narrative moves from Judea to Nazareth, where the Annunciation takes place. In this episode, the only two characters are the angel Gabriel and Mary. Joseph is not even mentioned. Then follows the story of the Visitation, when Mary goes to Judea to visit her relative Elizabeth. When she feels the child move in her womb, Elizabeth declares, "And why has this happened to me, that the mother of my

Lord comes to me?" (Luke 1:43). With these words Elizabeth becomes the first person in the Gospel of Luke to witness to the lordship of Jesus. It is during this visit that Mary expresses her praise in the *Magnificat*, which we have already discussed, and which, as we have seen, has revolutionary undertones. When Elizabeth gives birth to John, Zechariah also sings.

Here, in the two songs by Mary and Zechariah, we first encounter something that we shall see repeatedly as we continue to read Luke's two books: episodes and parables in which a man and a woman are presented in parallel fashion — in this case, by means of two canticles, one by Mary and the other by Zechariah.

When the day comes on which, in fulfillment of the Law, the child is to be redeemed by means of a sacrifice, he is taken to the temple, and there two people bear witness to him. One of them is Simeon, who pronounces the very brief song called the *Nunc dimittis* (Luke 2:29-32). But the other person is the elderly prophet Anna, who "never left the temple but worshiped there with fasting and prayer night and day"; she "began to praise God and to speak about the child to all who were looking for the redemption of Jerusalem" (Luke 2:36-38). Once again, a woman gives witness to Jesus.

At the beginning of his public ministry, in the sermon he gives in the synagogue after reading a passage from Isaiah, Jesus uses two people as illustrations of his main point: the widow of Zarephath in Elijah's time, and Naaman the leper in Elisha's time. Shortly thereafter, Luke tells us that Jesus healed many people, but the only one who is specifically mentioned is a woman, Peter's mother-in-law.

In chapter 6, we are told of Jesus' miracle in the synagogue: his healing of the man with the withered hand. At first, this episode seems to have no parallel. But as we continue reading, we find in chapter 13 the story of another miracle in the synagogue: Jesus' healing of the woman who was bent over. The two miracles are parallel: both take place on the Sabbath in a synagogue; both involve the healing of people with physical infirmities; both show that the issue is not the power of Jesus to heal, but rather whether it is lawful to perform such healings on the Sabbath; and both end with the confusion and wrath of the legalistic leaders, who place obedience to the Law above compassion.

Between these two miracles, there are others. There is, for instance, a pair of miracles in chapter 7. In the first of them, Jesus heals the servant of a centurion; in the second, he raises the son of the widow in Nain. And at the end of the same chapter there is the contrast already mentioned between the Pharisee who invites Jesus to dine with him and the sinful woman with the alabaster jar who anoints Jesus. While the Pharisee did not even wash Jesus' feet, the woman washes them with her tears and dries them with her hair.

In chapter 8 there is the story of Jairus, who comes to Jesus asking him to heal his only daughter, who is on the verge of death. But before Jesus can respond, he is interrupted by the woman with hemorrhages. It is only after Jesus heals this woman that he turns back to Jairus and his request. Thus, in these paired miracles, we have the healing of a sick woman wrapped within the healing of a man's daughter.

In chapter 10 this practice of telling stories of men and women in parallel fashion takes a particular turn, for the story about a man — or rather, about several men — is a parable, while the story about a woman — or rather, about two women — is a narrative. The first is the parable of the Good Samaritan and the second is the visit of Jesus to the home of Mary and Martha. Sometimes we preachers manipulate these two passages: if we deem that the church is not showing sufficient interest in the needy, we preach about the Good Samaritan; and if, on the contrary, it seems to us that the church is not sufficiently spiritual and does not study Scripture enough, we preach about Mary and Martha. In both cases, we forget the passage we have not selected. But the fact is that the parable of the Good Samaritan and the episode in the home of Mary and Martha are parallel, for both exalt someone who does the unexpected. The Samaritan helps the Jew in need, while the priest and the Levite pass by. The priest and the Levite have business to attend to, and they refuse the interruption of helping the man by the wayside. In the case of Mary and Martha, the latter is busy with the tasks traditionally assigned to women. In contrast, Mary, going against every social convention and apparently paying no attention to what was expected of a woman having a guest in her home, sits to listen to Jesus. When seen this way, the two passages point in the same direction, although in contrasting circumstances. Once again, the main character in the parable is a man, and in the narrative it is a woman. But both passages show that these people, a Samaritan and a woman, whose ability to be true disciples and followers of the Law might be doubted, are the ones who really understand and practice what God wills for them. Furthermore, we are told that Mary "sat at the Lord's feet and listened to what he was saying" (Luke 10:39) — which is not said about anyone else in the New Testament, including the Twelve.

In chapter 13 there are two parallel parables, both making the same point, but one about a man and the other about a woman. Jesus is seeking something with which to compare the reign of God, and he compares it first with a mustard seed that a man planted in a garden, and then with the leaven that a woman took and mixed with three measures of flour. If the man who planted the seed represents God, who has planted the seed of the reign, then the woman who placed the leaven in the flour is also a way of referring to God. And in chapter 15 there are again two parallel parables, one about a lost sheep and the other about a lost coin. In the first, God is like a man who is shepherding a hundred sheep and loses one. In the second, God is like a woman who has ten coins and loses one. Later on, in chapter 17, when Jesus wishes to stress the unexpected coming of the final day, and how then the just will be set aside from the wicked, he speaks first of "two" who seem to be a couple, although their gender is not indicated. Then he speaks of two women: "I tell you, on that night there will be two in one bed; one will be taken and the other left. There will be two women grinding meal together; one will be taken and the other left. Two will be in the field; one will be taken and the other left" (Luke 17:34-36). (Many manuscripts omit verse 36, about the two in the field. Did some copyist seek to complete the pairing by adding this, or was it in the original, and then omitted? It is impossible to know.)

At the beginning of chapter 21 there is a narrative which refers first to several men and then to a woman whom Jesus praises above the men in the story. The men are the rich, who were placing their money in the offering. The woman is a poor widow who was only able to give two small copper coins. Jesus praises the poor widow above the rich, saying that she gave more than they, for they gave out of their abundance, but she gave out of her poverty.

When we then move on to the book of Acts, we find that already in chapter 2, Peter quotes a passage from Joel in which it is foretold that God will pour out the Spirit on all flesh. In order to underscore the universal nature of this gift of the Spirit, the passage that Peter quotes has three pairs of recipients: sons/daughters; young men/ old men; male slaves/female slaves." Note that two of these pairs have to do with the gender of those mentioned. Thus, part of what the passage stresses is the equality between men and women when it comes to receiving the Spirit. In chapter 5, when we come to the story of Ananias and Sapphira, we see that, just as the gift of the Spirit is not limited to one gender, so also sin is not so limited, for the manner in which Luke tells the story shows that Ananias and Sapphira are equally sinful, and both pay the same price for their sin.

There is a similar parallelism in the miracles in Acts. At the very beginning of the book, Luke tells us that the Twelve "were constantly devoting themselves to prayer, together with certain women" (Acts 1:14). In chapter 9, as Peter preaches in the regions of Lydda and Joppa, we see first the healing of Aeneas and then the raising of Dorcas from the dead.

Throughout the book we repeatedly find references to men and women: those who believed were "both men and women" (Acts 5:14); in his persecution, Saul was "dragging off both men and women" (Acts 8:3); in Samaria, in response to Philip's preaching, both "men and women" were baptized (Acts 8:12); and Saul asked for letters to the synagogues at Damascus, so that he might seek "any who belonged to the Way, men or women" (Acts 9:2).

In summary, both in the Third Gospel and in Acts, and in the parables as well as in the narratives, we often find parallel references to men and women. In one case — in the stories of Jairus and of the woman with hemorrhages — the two stories are interwoven. Furthermore, such parallel references are not always positive, as may be seen in the story of Ananias and Sapphira. In some cases a contrast or comparison is made in which the men are shown to be wanting, as in the case of the Pharisee and the woman with the alabaster jar, and in the case of the offerings of the rich and the gift of the poor widow. But in most of these pairings, the passages refer in positive terms to both men and women. This may be seen in the parables of the lost sheep and the lost coin; in the stories of the man with the withered hand and the bent-over woman who go to the synagogue; in the miracles of Peter, who first heals Aeneas and then raises Dorcas; and in many other similar cases.

It is for this reason that one can safely say that among all the Evangelists it is Luke who pays the most attention to women and their place in the story he is telling.

★   ★   ★

But the place of women in Luke's narrative is not limited to these pairings. Both in the Third Gospel and in Acts there are several women leaders of the church who are specifically recognized. We often imagine that Jesus went from one place to another with the sole company of those disciples who would later be known as apostles. Such a picture may be compatible with the other Gospels, but not with Luke's Gospel. In Luke 8:1-3 we read the following:

> Soon afterwards he went on through cities and villages, proclaiming and bringing the good news of the kingdom of God. The twelve were with him, as well as some women who had been cured of evil spirits and infirmities: Mary, called Magdalene, from whom seven demons had gone out, and Joanna, the wife of Herod's steward Chuza, and Susanna, and many others, who provided for them out of their resources.

Once again Luke juxtaposes a group of men ("the Twelve") with another group of women. But in this case he does give us some names — although not all, for he declares that besides the three whom he names there were "many others." Those whose names are given are Mary Magdalene, Joanna, and Susanna. Mary Magdalene will appear again in the story of the Passion. In that context, all of the Four Evangelists attest to her presence at the foot of the cross. Luke is the only one who gives us more details about her, telling us that she had been healed of "seven demons." Since Luke also says that several of the other women had been healed of evil spirits and infirmities, it is common to think that in the case of Mary Magdalene this was not a physical infirmity, but rather a mental or psychological issue. For this reason she has traditionally been represented in art as a radically unkempt woman dressed in rags. Furthermore, in several languages, if one wants to say that another is not well-groomed, one says that the person "looks like a

Magdalene." From such a beginning, popular tradition has turned her into a particularly sinful woman, and has also identified her with the one who anointed the feet of Jesus with her tears and dried them with her hair. But there is no real foundation for such suppositions. All we know is that she was from Magdala (hence her name), that Jesus healed her, and that she followed him to the foot of the cross. Magdala was a city on the western coast of the Sea of Galilee, so Mary came from the region where Jesus began his ministry. There was in Magdala a flourishing fishing industry which produced an abundant quantity of the fish sauce that the Romans knew as *garum*. Accordingly, some have supposed that Mary had a connection with that industry. This may well have been the source of the wealth with which she supported Jesus and his companions.

Joanna, the second woman mentioned, does not appear again in the biblical record. Her husband was a steward to Herod Antipas — not the Herod of the slaughter of the innocents, but his successor. Luke does not tell us that she was a widow, and therefore the image presented seems to be that of a woman who has left her husband, a relatively powerful and wealthy man, in order to follow Jesus. Of the third woman mentioned, Susanna, all we know is her name. But the very fact that Luke mentions her without saying more about who she was seems to imply that he expected his readers to know her, and that therefore she must have been an important person in the ancient church.

In any case, Luke tells us that three particular women and many others traveled with Jesus and the Twelve, and that they "provided for them out of their resources." This implies that they were relatively well-to-do women, and results in a very different picture than we usually imagine. Jesus and his followers were not simply going from place to place and living on the alms of those whom they met, as the first Franciscans imagined and imitated. Rather, it was the women who paid their bills!

The story of these women does not end here, for Luke as well as the other Evangelists tell us that Mary Magdalene and several other women were at the cross, and that they were more faithful than any of the men, except John. Mark and Matthew seem to acknowledge at that late moment that these women had provided support for Jesus and his companions. Matthew tells us that "they had provided for him" (Matt. 27:55). And Mark also says that when Jesus was in Galilee, these women "used to follow him and provided for him" (Mark 15:41). While Matthew and Mark may suggest that these women were servants of Jesus and his companions, Luke makes it very clear that these women actually provided for their support.

We now come to the story of Jesus' burial and resurrection. All the Evangelists agree that it was the women who first learned of the Resurrection. In Mark, the angel at the tomb tells the women to go and tell the other disciples what they know, but they "said nothing to anyone, for they were afraid" (Mark 16:8). Shortly thereafter, Jesus appears to Mary Magdalene, and she is the one who carries the news to the others. In Matthew, it is Mary Magdalene and "the other Mary" who first go to the tomb, and are told by the angel to let the others know of Jesus' resurrection (Matt. 1:1-10). In John, Mary Magdalene goes alone to the tomb and first learns of the resurrection of the Lord. In Luke, something different takes place. Joseph of Arimathea lays Jesus' body in a fresh tomb, and "the women who had come with him from Galilee" see the tomb and "how [Jesus'] body was laid" (Luke 23:55). When they return to the tomb with spices and ointments, they encounter two angels who tell them that Christ is risen, and the women take this news "to the eleven, and to all the rest" (Luke 24:1-9). Luke is the only one to name three of these women and to emphatically recognize them and the others as the news-bearers: "Now it was Mary Magdalene, Joanna, Mary the mother of James, and the other women with them who told this to the apostles" (v. 10). To sum up: all the Evangelists agree that Mary

Magdalene, the same woman who has gotten such bad press in the Christian tradition, was the first messenger or one of the first messengers to announce Jesus' resurrection. But only Luke has taken care to tell us at an earlier point who Mary Magdalene and these other women were, and how they gave economic support to Jesus and his companions. The others simply present Mary Magdalene suddenly at the foot of the cross.

There is a parallel between the passage in Luke 8 about the women who supported Jesus with their goods and what Luke tells us in Acts 16 about Lydia of Thyatira. According to this narrative, Lydia was a seller of purple, one of the most expensive dyes in antiquity — so costly that a purple cloak was considered a sign of great wealth and power. Therefore, Lydia must have been a woman of means. In Philippi, she was the one who believed the witness of Paul and his companions and invited them to dwell in her house. It is well-known that Paul did not cherish the idea of taking favors from his followers, and therefore insisted on supporting himself by the work of his hands. But in this case he accepted Lydia's invitation. This woman was not only rich and hospitable, but also strong, as Luke hints by saying that "she prevailed upon us" (Acts 16:15). Lydia was the beginning of the church in Philippi, and therefore it is not surprising that later this particular church was known for its support of Paul's project of collecting an offering for the poor in Jerusalem.

After Paul and Silas left Lydia's home, they traveled to Thessalonica, which we read about in Acts 17. In the Jewish synagogue there, Paul taught "on three sabbath days," and Luke tells us that among those who believed there were "a great many of the devout Greeks and not a few of the leading women" (Acts 17:3-4). He also tells us that in Beroea many believed, and that among them were "not a few Greek women" (Acts 17:12). And in Athens, where Paul's success was not as remarkable, among those who believed were

"Dionysius the Areopagite and a woman named Damaris" (Acts 17:34) — a woman whom later tradition made the wife of Dionysius, apparently because it was unseemly that a woman would be able to decide to follow Jesus on her own account.

In Acts 18, Luke introduces in his narrative a Jewish couple who had been forced to leave Rome when Emperor Claudius expelled the Jews from the city. The two are commonly known as "Aquila and Priscilla," but in Acts they appear almost always as "Priscilla and Aquila." This "Priscilla" is the same "Prisca" that has such an important place in Paul's epistles to the Romans and to the Corinthians. In Acts, Luke tells us that when the Alexandrian Jew Apollos arrived in Ephesus and showed himself to be an eloquent and powerful preacher, but not quite correct on certain points of doctrine, it was Priscilla and Aquila — in that order — who instructed him in the way of the Lord. In other words, Luke tells us that Priscilla was a professor of theology!

Finally, in order to complete the picture of Luke's narratives, we must consider the vision of the Macedonian man and its outcome in Philippi. The vision takes place in Troas, on the eastern side of the Bosphorus. In his introduction to this episode, Luke tells us how Paul and his companions came to Troas. He explains that the Holy Spirit would not allow them to speak the Word in the province of Asia; they then tried to go to the neighboring province of Bithynia, but once again the Spirit hindered them. So they went to Troas, apparently wondering which direction to take from there, when Paul had the vision of the Macedonian man. It is important to note that the Greek word employed here, *aner*, underscores the fact that the person is male. This man asks Paul to "come over to Macedonia and help us" (Acts 16:9). Obeying the vision, Paul and his companions make haste, taking a straight course from Troas to Samothrace and then Neapolis. From there they go to Philippi, which Luke describes as "a leading city of the district" (Acts 16:12). In Philippi they tried to follow their usual procedure in cities: they went in search of a synagogue where Jews would be gathered, in order to preach to them first. But in Philippi there was no synagogue; apparently Jews in that city used to gather on the Sabbath by the river on the outskirts of the city. So Paul and his companions went there. In all of this, they are responding to the invitation of the Macedonian man. But what they find by the river is not a synagogue, which required a certain number of males in order to be formally constituted, but a group of women! It was these women whom they addressed. Among them was the already mentioned Lydia of Thyatira, who was converted and baptized and became a pillar in what seems to have been Paul's favorite church.

There is a measure of irony in this story. The Spirit sent Paul a vision of a man, and what he found in Philippi was a group of women! What is often said about Paul's anti-feminine prejudices is probably at least an exaggeration, and perhaps even an error. But if Paul did have such prejudices, which were common in that time, Luke presents the Holy Spirit as overcoming them by sending Paul the vision of the Macedonian man, when what he is to find in Philippi is a group of women.

Many other examples could be given. One of them is the reference in Acts 21:9 to Philip's four daughters who had the gift of prophecy. All of this makes it clear that the matter of gender and of the strength and courage of women as part of the church is a theme of Luke's interest. The repeated pairings of stories and parables about men and women, the fact that the other Evangelists seem to ignore that it was the women who financially supported the ministry of Jesus, and the presence of strong women such as Mary Magdalene, Lydia, and Priscilla are proof enough.

★   ★   ★

Such is the theme of gender in Luke. But it would be wrong to ignore what happened to this theme almost as soon as Luke published his books. This may be seen particularly in the textual history of Acts. As is frequently the case with ancient books, Acts has come to us through different manuscript traditions — in this case, mainly two. These are usually known as the Alexandrine or common text and the Western text. In the case of Acts, more than in other books of the New Testament, the differences are notable. Scholars agree on the one hand that the Alexandrine text is closer to the original and, on the other hand, that the Western text was produced just a few decades after the original.

(I should note in passing that, quite apart from the matter of gender, the Western text shows several attempts to correct Luke. Thus, for instance, the Western text of Luke's Gospel shows a prejudice against Jews. This is particularly true in the story of the Passion, where Luke (in the Alexandrine or common text) distinguishes between "the people," who are mostly favorable to Jesus and his disciples, and those in authority — the guards of the temple, the Sadducees — who are the ones plotting against Jesus and having him crucified. The Western text, by underplaying that distinction between the people and those in authority, tends to blame the Jews in general, and not only their leaders.)

Now back to the subject of gender. From that early time when the Western text was produced, one can detect efforts to weaken the manner in which Acts presents matters of gender. Thus, for instance, the original text of Acts usually refers to "Priscilla and Aquila," in that order. The one exception is a case in which grammar requires placing "Aquila" first. But the Western text inverts that order so that now "Priscilla and Aquila" becomes "Aquila and Priscilla." In Acts 17:12, where the common text says that among those who believed in Beroea there were "not a few Greek women and men of high standing," implying that both men and women were "of high standing," the Western text says that those who believed were "women and not a few men of high standing." In some cases, the Western text simply ignores the role of women — as in Acts 17:34, where the name of Damaris is omitted.

But it was not only the redactor of the Western text who, intentionally or not, sought to weaken what Luke and Acts say about women. The same has happened throughout history. In the case of Priscilla and Aquila, it is not only the Western text that inverts the order. Thus, it is quite common in the church today to refer to "Aquila and Priscilla," in that order. Likewise, we often hear about God as the Father of the prodigal son, but not as the woman who loses a coin, or the woman who hides a bit of leaven in the flour. When we think about Jesus walking by the fields in Galilee on his way to Jerusalem, we imagine him accompanied by his twelve disciples, but we forget Mary Magdalene, Susanna, Joanna, and the "many others" who not only walked with him, but also covered the expenses of the group.

As a result, much of what Luke has to say on the matter of gender lies hidden under layers of interpretation that we have received from earlier generations. It is therefore urgent, for the good of the church, that we continue unearthing what has been hidden. In this task, the many women who today are devoted to the careful study of the biblical text are making an important contribution.

FIVE

Luke and Salvation

To you is born this day in the city of David a Savior,
who is the Messiah, the Lord.

Luke 2:11

W E ARE SO ACCUSTOMED to speaking of Jesus as "our Savior" that we hardly notice that this is typically Lukan and Pauline terminology. Of the three Synoptic Gospels, only Luke speaks of Jesus as "Savior." John gives him this title only once, when the Samaritans who have been moved by the witness of the Samaritan woman declare that "this is truly the Savior of the world" (John 4:42). Likewise, the word *salvation*, which is so important for us and for the whole church, does not appear in Matthew or in Mark. John uses the word only once, again in the story of the Samaritan woman, to whom Jesus declares that "salvation is from the Jews" (John 4:22). In contrast, both the title of "Savior" and the word *salvation* appear repeatedly in the Gospel of Luke and in Acts. Therefore, in order to understand Luke's theology, we must discuss the matter of "salvation."

*   *   *

The Hebrew text of the Old Testament uses several words that the Septuagint — the translation of the Old Testament into Greek — then translated as *soteria*, meaning "salvation"; *sozein*, meaning "to save"; and *soter*, meaning "Savior." This multitude of words in Hebrew is a reminder of the many meanings included in this notion, and of how difficult it is to include these meanings in the words *salvation, saving,* and *savior,* all of which are derived from a single root. In the Old Testament, these words are employed to refer to God and to divine action. For that reason they are basic to the narrative of the Old Testament. In the Psalms alone, the various terms that may be translated as *salvation* appear more than sixty times; they appear about thirty times in Isaiah. In most of these cases, "salvation" is an action of the God who is "Savior." In their etymology, several of the Hebrew words that today we translate as *salvation* mean "widening," "amplifying," and therefore "liberating, ridding of oppression and bondage." They do not always — or even usually — refer to eternal life. Nor do they have the eschatological dimensions which today we give to the word *salvation.* The main saving act of God in the Old Testament is the liberation from the yoke of Egypt, and it is to that liberation that many of the texts which speak of God as Savior refer. In addition, a "savior" quite frequently is one who liberates the people from an alien yoke. For instance, in 2 Kings 13:5 we are told that "the LORD gave Israel a savior [unnamed], so that they escaped from the hand of the Arameans." And in Judges 13:5 Samson's mother is told that her son shall begin to save Israel from the Philistines. But in these cases, and in many similar ones that could be cited, these acts of salvation are a reflection of the great saving act of God, which is the deliverance from Egypt. In the Old Testament, therefore, salvation is the action of God and of God's servants in freeing Israel from slavery and subjection to the Egyptians, Philistines, Syrians, Babylonians, and all the threatening neighboring nations. Salvation is also the divine action protecting Israel in the field of battle, giving it victory over its enemies.

In other cases, Hebrew words that the Septuagint translates as *salvation* and *savior* have to do with redemption. Redemption is an act by which one recovers what has come to belong to another. A relative who has been sold as a slave may be redeemed by means of a payment to the master. In the case of properties, this may be seen, for instance, in chapter 4 of the book of Ruth, where Boaz formally discusses with a relative, before witnesses, who is to redeem the land that had belonged to the now-deceased Elimelech: "So I thought I would tell you of it, and say: Buy it in the presence of those sitting here, and in the presence of the elders of my people. If you will redeem it, redeem it; but if you will not, tell me, so that I may know; for there is no one prior to you to redeem it, and I come after you" (Ruth 4:4). This passage makes it clear that not everyone can be a redeemer, for one has to have certain rights to a property. In this case, Boaz is kin to Elimelech, and so can redeem the land. In an earlier chapter of this book, while discussing the presentation of Jesus in the temple, we saw that the Law made every firstborn within Israel God's property, which had to be redeemed by means of a sacrifice. Thus, Joseph and Mary take Jesus to the temple in order to redeem him through the sacrifice of two birds. Thus, redemption takes place when someone who has a certain right to something that is currently in the hands of another reclaims it. This is what is implied frequently when the Old Testament speaks of God as "redeemer." When the prophet Isaiah says that "your Redeemer is the Holy One of Israel" (Isa. 41:14), this means that Israel properly belongs to God, and that therefore in delivering the people from the yoke of Egyptians, Babylonians, and others, God is simply reclaiming what is God's possession.

At this point, it is important to note that among all the Gospels, the words *redemption* and *to redeem* appear only in Luke — the same Gospel that is noted for its use of the title "Savior" and the word *salvation*. The notion itself is not totally alien to the other Gospels, for in Matthew 20:28 and the parallel text in Mark 10:45, we are told that Jesus has come "to give his life a ransom for many." Even so, the theme of redemption, just like that of salvation, is typically Lukan.

Turning once again to the Greek that is employed in the Septuagint and in the New Testament, what this means is that the words that today we translate as *saving, salvation,* and *savior* can have — and often do have — several meanings. These meanings include liberating from oppression, liberating from the power of death, restoring health, and so on. Therefore, upon encountering the word *soteria,* translators have to decide whether to render it as *salvation* or as *healing,* for there is no single word in English that includes both meanings. Taking all this into account as we examine first the Gospel of Luke and then the book of Acts, we shall see that when in these books we find the word *salvation,* it refers not only to what we today understand as "salvation," but may also refer to the restoration of health, to liberation from an enemy or a threat, and to the reclaiming of what properly belongs to God.

★   ★   ★

In the words quoted at the beginning of this chapter, the shepherds are told that "to you is born this day in the city of David a Savior, who is the Messiah, the Lord" (Luke 2:11). Today, when we as Christians read these words, we immediately know that what is being announced is the birth of the One who will save us from sin and death. But the meaning is different if we read these words as the shepherds would have understood them. Luke tells us that Joseph and Mary had gone to Bethlehem in response to an edict from Augustus Caesar "that all the world should be registered" in a census (Luke 2:1). It is easy for us to think that Luke was speaking of the kind of census that is now taken periodically in most nations — but it was much more than that. It was a total inventory not only of the inhabitants, but also of their lands, their flocks, and any other possessions they had. The purpose of such a census was not only to determine how many people there were, but also to determine what taxes they were able to pay. Accordingly, this census by Augustus Caesar was regarded with disfavor by the peoples under Roman rule — among them, Israel — and this led to a tense situation. Those shepherds keeping their watch by night over their flocks knew that those flocks were being counted, and that a good part of them would be claimed by the publicans and the entire system of taxation. One wonders what these shepherds discussed as they watched over their flocks! One may well imagine that they weren't talking about the stars above or about the weather, but rather about how hard it was for them simply to survive. Then, suddenly, an angel appeared before them, and they were surrounded by a great light.

In order to understand the drama of that moment, we need to imagine what it might have been like to live in a nation that was oppressive and exploitative. A group of shepherds sitting around a fire at night might not have discussed the government itself, but they would have known that it was to be feared and that they had to be careful. And then, suddenly, someone appeared in the midst of them, and they were surrounded by a great light! The situation would have been frightening. So it isn't surprising that Luke tells us that "they were terrified" (Luke 2:9). It is in response to that fear that the angel speaks these oft-quoted words: "Do not be afraid; for see — I am bringing you good news of great joy for all the people: to you is born this day in the city of David a Savior, who is the Messiah, the Lord" (Luke 2:10-11). Today we know that this reference to a savior has eternal dimensions, that Luke is referring to an eternal salvation. But for those shepherds, mention of such a savior would immediately have reminded them of the other saviors of whom the Bible spoke: Moses, Joshua, Samson . . .

All of this may make us feel smug, make us feel that we understand what was taking place better than did those shepherds. This may well be the case. But perhaps we should also stop for a moment to consider the possibility that, in setting aside those other dimensions of the meaning of the word *Savior*, we may be losing something of what Luke is trying to tell us.

At this point it may be helpful to remember what was said earlier about typology. In biblical typology there is an entire chain of "salvations," all of which are types or figures of the salvation that is to come in Jesus Christ. The Exodus from Egypt stands out among all these events of salvation that point as signs to their culmination in Jesus. This type, this pattern of the action of God as Savior, appears repeatedly in the Old Testament, in all the struggles of the children of Israel as they try to attain and keep their freedom, as well as in their return from the Babylonian Exile. As already stated, the liberation that takes place in the Exodus is the pattern that the prophet Isaiah later takes up as "a voice of one calling in the wilderness," announcing the return from the Exile. All of this also points to another voice crying in the wilderness: John's voice, announcing the arrival of full salvation in the person of Jesus. Furthermore, between the Exodus and the Exile, and between the Exile and John the Baptist, there are dozens of liberating actions, of saving works of God in which the children of Israel can once again acknowledge the work of the God who led them out of Egypt and out of Babylon.

All of this means that when a pattern reaches its climax in Jesus, this cannot be understood fully without the earlier manifestations of the same pattern. This is why Christians repeatedly rejected every attempt to leave the Old Testament aside, as if now the New Testament were enough. No! The God who comes to us in Jesus Christ for salvation is the same God who intervened repeatedly in the history of Israel, also for their salvation — although "for their salvation" in a narrower sense than what is found in the New Testament.

Therefore, when the shepherds heard that a savior had been born unto them, no doubt they understood this announcement as one more instance of God bringing forth those who saved Israel from Egypt, from the Philistines, and from Babylonia. This does not mean that their understanding was wrong, but simply that it was still incomplete, for they did not know the full meaning of the salvation which Jesus brings. Something similar happened with the disciples of Jesus, who did not seem to understand the nature of his mission, and at the very moment of his ascension into heaven were still asking him when he would restore the Davidic kingdom, when he would free them from the yoke of Rome. Israel's liberation from Egypt was God's action; David's kingdom was God's action; the return from Babylon was God's action. The fact that now the New Testament speaks of liberation in a wider sense, of a reign of God, and of a permanent return to God does not deny the action of God in that first liberation, in that Davidic kingdom, or in that first return. On the contrary, all those divine actions help us understand more fully the action of God in Jesus Christ and through the Holy Spirit.

So the shepherds, as mentioned above, had an incomplete understanding of the angel's announcement of a savior, because they knew only the various instances of salvation in the Old Testament. But when we come to our own situation, we may have an opposite problem because of how we view salvation in the New Testament. If the way in which we understand salvific events there makes it incompatible with the great salvific actions of God in the Old Testament, then we, like the shepherds, have an incomplete and deficient understanding of salvation. In other words, we have repeatedly heard that we must read the Old Testament in the light of the New, and that is true. But it is equally true that we must learn how to read the New Testament in the light of the Old.

*   *   *

There is no doubt that the New Testament stresses the promise of eternal life, and that salvation includes that life. But this does not mean that salvation has to do only with life after death. Just as, in the Old Testament, salvation has to do with defense against oppressors, with liberation from injustice, with the freedom and health of the people, so too in the New Testament it has to do with the present order, with the manner in which people and families shape and live their lives.

Another passage in the Gospel of Luke that allows us to understand the full meaning of salvation is the one about Zacchaeus, when Jesus tells him, "Today salvation has come to this house" (Luke 19:9). Certainly, this means that there is a place for Zacchaeus in the eternal life of God's reign. But it is important to note that Jesus' declaration follows a decision on the part of Zacchaeus: "Look, half of my possessions, Lord, I will give to the poor; and if I have defrauded anyone of anything, I will pay back four times as much" (Luke 19:8). In other words, Jesus tells Zacchaeus that, with his promise to practice mercy and do justice, salvation has come to his house. And we can see that this is not a salvation for the morrow, not one that will take place only after death, because Jesus says that "*today* salvation has come to this house." And, while the words of Zacchaeus before Jesus' announcement help us understand the matter of salvation, we are also helped by the rest of what Jesus says — namely, that salvation has come "because he too is a son of Abraham" (Luke 19:9), which indicates that this salvation is not something radically new, but is the continuation of the saving work of God throughout the history of Israel, the fulfillment of the promises made to Abraham.

The next time the word *salvation* appears in the writings of Luke is in Acts 4:12: "There is salvation in no one else, for there is no other name under heaven given among mortals by which we must be saved." This passage has been much discussed, particularly in dealing with the question of whether one who is not a Christian may inherit eternal life. Similarly, it is employed to declare that there is no other way to reach God but through faith in Jesus.

While all of this may be true, let us leave it aside for the moment, and read the passage again within the context of what Luke is narrating. We need to understand what has taken place, the context in which Peter pronounces these words. Peter has healed the lame man who was by the temple gate. The man, grateful for what has been done, goes into the temple not only walking, but leaping and praising God. The people are astonished, and while Peter and John are responding to their amazement by proclaiming the message of Jesus, the priests, the captain of the temple guard, and the Sadducees come to arrest them and take them to jail.

On the following day, Peter and John are taken before the leadership of the Jews and are asked, "By what power or by what name did you do this?" (Acts 4:7). Peter responds with a speech that is one more instance of the great reversal which we have already discussed:

> Rulers of the people and elders, if we are questioned today because of a good deed done to someone who was sick and are asked how this man has been healed, let it be known to all of you, and to all the people of Israel, that this man is standing before you in good health by the name of Jesus Christ of Nazareth, whom you crucified, whom God raised from the dead. This Jesus is "the stone that was rejected by you, the builders; it has become the cornerstone." There is salvation in no one else, for there is no other name under heaven given among mortals by which we must be saved. (Acts 4:8-12)

It is not necessary to dwell on the manner in which this passage deals again with the great reversal. It is sufficient to note that Jesus, who was crucified, has risen from the dead, that the stone which was rejected has become the cornerstone.

What does merit much more careful analysis is the subject that is being discussed. The trial has nothing to do with eternal salvation, but rather with the authority or the name by which the man has been healed. What Peter and John are asked is "By what power or by what name did you do this?" — in other words, How did you heal this man? Peter knows exactly what the subject under discussion is and what is being asked, for he himself states it again: "We are questioned today because of a good deed done to someone who was sick and are asked how this man has been healed." His answer to the question is that this has been done by the power of the one whom his audience crucified and who has now risen from the dead: "this man is standing before you in good health by the name of Jesus." All of this leads to this very well-known declaration: "There is salvation in no one else, for there is no other name under heaven given among mortals by which we must be saved." When we read these words of Peter in context, it is surprising that, in a discussion about the healing of a lame man, Peter goes on to speak of eternal salvation. What is the relationship between the two?

The answer is in what was said above: that in Greek the same word that refers to eternal salvation may also refer to the healing of a sick person. While the title of "savior" and the word *salvation* do not appear frequently in the other Gospels, the word *sozein*, meaning "to save or to heal," does appear frequently, although most commonly in the sense of healing. Thus, when Jesus heals a sick person, *sozein* is the word that is employed: Jesus heals or saves them, for the two meanings come from the same word.

This means that the words of Peter may be translated in two ways: as is most commonly done, as referring to salvation and being saved into eternal life, or, with equal faithfulness to the Greek text, as "there is healing in no one else, for there is no other name

under heaven given among mortals by which we must be healed."
Both translations are correct, and it is not necessary to reject one
in favor of the other. What is important to realize is that they are
both equally valid, and that when we do not consider both of them,
we may well be missing something important not only in the text
itself but also in the biblical understanding of salvation.

Since the traditional translation, "There is salvation in no one
else," is well-known, it is not necessary to say much about its significance for Christian faith. Quite clearly, it means something similar to what Jesus says in John 14:6: "No one comes to the Father
except through me." But it is also important to look at the other
translation — that there is no healing in any other name than that
of Jesus.

Our first reaction may well be that this other translation reduces
the importance of what the text says, for instead of speaking about
eternal life, it refers to physical health. But if we take it seriously,
this other translation points to unsuspected dimensions in the
power of Jesus. Peter is not only saying that the man has been
healed by this power. He is saying that all healing takes place by
the same power. If we take it quite literally, the text means that if
someone is healed in Manchuria, this is the work of the same Jesus
Christ whom Peter and John proclaim. It means that if today an
unbelieving doctor heals someone, that healing is also the work
of the same Jesus Christ, even though the doctor may not know it
or may even deny it. It means that the same Jesus who is the source
of every salvation is also the source of every healing.

This is important, for one of the shortcomings of the church
through the centuries has been forgetting the cosmic dimensions
of this Jesus Christ whom we proclaim. We seek to limit his power
and turn to our own reach and power. We imagine that Jesus heals,
yes, but only where we take him. But what Peter is saying is that the
reach of Jesus is much wider than the reach of the church: "There

is healing in no one else, for there is no other name under heaven given among mortals by which we must be healed." (At this point, it is important to remember that the "name" of Jesus in this context is not the mere combination of the letters J e s u s, but is rather the very person and authority of Jesus. What is meant is not that to be healed one has to say "Jesus," but rather that every healing and every salvation take place through the power and the mercy of Jesus.)

Interestingly, this passage in Acts is parallel to another passage in John with which we rarely relate it. In John 1:9 we are told that the Word of God is "the true light, which enlightens everyone." As many Christians throughout the centuries have declared, this means that every light, every knowledge, every truth comes from this Word who was incarnate in Jesus Christ. Ancient Christians understood that all knowledge — from the mere assertion that two and two make four to the discovery of the greatest mysteries of life and the universe — comes through the Word of God; that in this sense, any truth is Christian truth, for its ultimate source is none other than the Word that became incarnate in Jesus. Thus, what John 1 tells us about knowledge and truth, Acts 4 tells us about health and well-being. There is no health, no well-being, no truth, no existence that is not a gift of this Jesus, apart from whom there is neither salvation nor health.

★   ★   ★

There are many other texts in Acts about the salvation that Jesus offers — salvation in the fullest sense of the word. One of them which we often miss, but which is fundamental for understanding the mission of the church, is in Acts 16. This chapter includes two well-known narratives: the vision of the Macedonian man, which we have already discussed, and the story of the jailer in Philippi. Let it be said in passing that the jailer also asks, "Sirs, what must I do to be saved?," and it is not clear whether he is referring to eternal salvation or to being saved from the consequences of what has just taken place. What we often forget is the reason why Paul and Silas are in jail. A young girl with a spirit of divination had been following Paul and his companions, shouting. "These men are slaves of the Most High God, who proclaim to you a way of salvation" (v. 17). There is no doubt that what the girl is saying is true. Paul and his companions are certainly servants of the Most High God, and they announce the way of salvation. But even so, Paul is annoyed and says to the spirit in the girl, "I order you in the name of Jesus Christ to come out of her" (v. 18). It is then that the owners of the girl, whose business has been interrupted, seize Paul and Silas and take them before the authorities, accusing them of disturbing the city.

How is it that Paul can be annoyed when what the girl is saying is true? Her proclamation might be of great benefit for the evangelizing work of Paul and his companions. If the way of salvation were purely spiritual (relating only to salvation from death and to eternal life), if it were only a matter of doctrines and beliefs, Paul should rejoice that this girl is validating their preaching. We might expect him to feel that the girl's spirit of divination will convince many to be converted. But Paul is actually annoyed and tells the spirit to leave the girl. This apparently strange attitude is due precisely to the fact that salvation is much more than a ticket to heaven. Biblical salvation is an integral salvation. It is a matter that has to do not only with liberation from the power of death, but also with liberation from every oppressive power. The girl who announces that Paul and Silas are messengers of the true God is herself subject to a demonic power. The girl who declares that what Paul and his companions announce is the way of salvation is enslaved both by that spirit and by her owners, who exploit her oppression. If Paul and Silas are truly announcing the way of salvation, and this is an integral salvation, then the preachers of that way may not be satisfied with having people believe them, but must do everything possible to announce and to practice that great salvation — that great healing — which is a gift and a promise of God. If, on the contrary, they are content with the girl's witness, what they announce will not be truly the salvation that the Bible proclaims and Jesus brings. In these events, Paul and his companions are offering a better witness than that of the girl, for they are pointing to good news that will include the whole of life, both eternal life and the present life.

⋆   ⋆   ⋆

Those Christians today who emphasize the healing power of God are making an important contribution to the discovery of Luke's theology as well as of the biblical vision of an integral salvation. This does not mean, however, that God will heal all who are ill. Nor does it mean that if one is healed and the other is not, this is because one had faith and the other did not. God did not free Paul from the thorn in his flesh, or Jesus from the agony of the cross. But it does mean that while we proclaim the message of salvation in the sense of eternal life, we also have to proclaim the same message in the sense of liberation from every power of evil.

Unfortunately, for several decades many Christians have been hopelessly mired in debates about whether one should begin with material help to the needy, hoping that they will come to believe the gospel, or one should simply preach the gospel. The truth is that purely material help is incomplete, and that a purely spiritual gospel is also incomplete. Any gospel preaching that does not condemn evil wherever it might be and seek to correct it will be wrongheaded, just as Paul and Silas would have been wrong to be content with the declaration of that young girl in Philippi. If it is true that there is health in no other name than that of Jesus Christ, then all health is Christian, and therefore all health is part of the mission of the church.

Furthermore, what is said about illness and disease must be said about every other form of oppression and dehumanization. If we are to be faithful to the biblical view of salvation as an integral reality, we cannot simply tolerate any evil as long as it does not impede our preaching — and much less are we to support those evils that might make our preaching easier.

Since our interest here is to attain a fuller vision of Luke's theology, there are two points that must be underscored. First, it is important to note that the theme of salvation appears from the very beginning to the very end of his work — at the beginning in the angel's message to the shepherds; and at the end, in the last words of Paul: "Let it be known to you then that this salvation of God has been sent to the Gentiles; they will listen" (Acts 28:28). And second, we must stress the fact that this salvation is integral, that it includes both the soul and the body, both matter and the spirit, both the individual and the community.

This is Luke's vision of salvation and the vision by which we live. It is a vision that Peter declares before the leadership of Israel: "There is salvation in no one else, for there is no other name under heaven given among mortals by which we must be saved."

SIX

Food and Drink in Luke's Theology

Look, a glutton and a drunkard.

Luke 7:34

COMMENTARIES HAVE OFTEN POINTED out that, much more frequently than in any of the other Gospels, in the Gospel of Luke we find Jesus eating. And that there are many other references to food and drink. One commentary offers a list of sixty such references — which comes out to about two and a half references per chapter! So, clearly, the theme of eating and drinking is not peripheral in the Gospel of Luke; rather, it is an element important to the way in which this Evangelist wishes us to understand his message.

It is important to point out, however, that a good number of the banquets and meals that Luke mentions appear also in Matthew and Mark (although not all of them). On this point there is a difference between the writers of the three Synoptic Gospels and John, who seems to be more interested in drink than in food, and who does not even tell us of Jesus' last supper with his disciples before his crucifixion. And, also in contrast with Luke, the meals that John describes in more detail are not at the homes of Pharisees and tax collectors, nor are they occasions for debate with scribes or Pharisees. Leaving aside the wedding at Cana in John 2, where the wine is more important than the food, there are two meals mentioned in the Gospel of John. In chapter 12, during a banquet in her own home, Mary of Bethany anoints Jesus with perfume, and this leads to the protest of Judas. Then, in chapter 21, after his resurrection, Jesus eats with his disciples. Therefore, in dealing with the subject of food and drink in Luke, we must remember that the same theme appears also in Matthew and Mark, though not with the same emphasis. And we must also remember that in John there are frequent references to Jesus himself as food and drink, but there are few narratives about specific meals.

Eating and drinking are not only a physical necessity, but also an important element in the fabric of any society. Even to this day, when we sit together with someone at a table, this implies some sort of relationship. It may be a matter of friendship, of business, or of simply trying to get to know each other better. But in any case, sitting with another at a table is both a sign and a way to create and develop relationships.

This has been true in every society through the ages. Our present word *companion* comes from Latin roots which mean "common" and "bread." Therefore, a companion is someone with whom we break bread. In some societies in which violence is frequent and life is unstable, sharing bread is a sign of friendship or at least of respect. Thus, if one is passing through another's land and breaks bread with them, this means that there will be no hostilities. Also, we should remember that in every society, great occasions are frequently celebrated with a meal. If someone is having a birthday, we gather to eat together, or at least to share a cake or a special dessert. When a couple is celebrating an important point in their relationship, such as fifty years of marriage, it is customary to hold a banquet. When we wish to honor someone, we frequently do so with a special lunch or dinner. And when there is a wedding, very often the celebration includes a meal.

With some variations, all of this was also done in ancient times. This is the reason why, throughout the Bible (not only in the Gospel of Luke), there are abundant instances of celebrations consisting of meals. For instance, in the parable of the prodigal son, the father celebrates the return of the wayward son with a feast. Likewise, when the Bible speaks of the final day, it often describes that as the great feast or banquet of the marriage of the Lamb. In ancient times, meals were also occasions during which to discuss the most profound subjects. Today we have lost much of this meaning in our meals, mostly for two reasons, both rooted in haste. One of them is the popularity of what we call "fast food." We run into a place like McDonald's and order a hamburger with French fries, and ten minutes later we leave, supposedly having had a meal. The second reason is that, even when we eat at home, we often do so quickly. Most of the time we have something to do until suppertime, and something to do immediately afterwards — perhaps watching a favorite television program, preparing for classes for the next day, or going to church. The result is that, even at home, hardly ever do we linger at the table.

⋆   ⋆   ⋆

Things were very different in antiquity. In classical Greece, it was customary to celebrate *symposia.* Today a symposium is a program, sometimes lasting several days, in which people gather to discuss a theme of common interest to them. But the word *symposium,* like *companion,* also has roots that point to its origin. One of these roots is the Greek particle *syn,* which means "jointly" — suggested today by words like *synergy.* The second root is a verb meaning "to drink," *potizein,* which is the root of our word *potable.* These words hint at what a symposium used to be: a gathering in which a group of guests, reclining as they ate and drank, discussed a philosophical subject. Among the *Dialogues* of Plato there is one called the *Symposium,* in which seven people gather to discuss the subject of love. Among them is what today we would call a lawyer, as well as a physician, a poet, a comedic playwright, and Socrates, Plato's teacher. Each of them brings to the conversation a speech in praise of love, and finally Socrates points out that true love is love for wisdom — that is, philosophy.

In the Gospel of Luke, there are indications that at least some of the meals that Jesus attends are this sort of extensive conversation with guests who are reclining at a table. For instance, when in Luke 5:29 the NRSV tells us that there were people "sitting at the table," the Greek verb actually means that they were reclining at the table. The same is true in eleven other cases in Luke (Luke 7:36, 49; 9:14, 15; 11:37; 12:37; 13:29; 14:10; 22:14, 27; 24:30). Therefore, when we read in Luke of an incident that takes place when someone invites Jesus to dine, we are not to imagine that this would be a fast meal lasting a few minutes. Jesus isn't simply traveling along the road, hungry, when somebody invites him in for a quick bite. He is usually invited to rather prolonged dinners, during which the guests, reclining at the table, have the time to discuss subjects at length. And these dinners are also mostly formal occasions, during which certain customs and practices are expected to inform the behavior of both the host and the guests.

The first of these banquets or symposia appears in Luke in chapter 5, where Levi, a tax collector, follows Jesus and invites him to dinner. As Luke puts it, "Levi gave a great banquet for him in his house; and there was a large crowd of tax collectors and others sitting at the table with them" (Luke 5:29). Tax collectors were despised by all peoples who were subject to Roman rule, but particularly by Jews. The manner in which the Romans collected taxes was based on a census such as the one that Augustus Caesar had ordered, on which basis the royal treasury knew the resources of each province or region, and therefore what could be expected from it by way of taxes. But, rather than collecting those taxes directly, Roman authorities simply sold the right to collect taxes in a particular province to an entrepreneur. That entrepreneur then subleased those rights to others, and these to others, down to the ones who actually collected the taxes. Jointly, all of these investors and collectors of taxes were known as "publicans," because they served a treasury that was supposed to be public. Since each of these various levels of administration required a profit, publicans found that they needed to collect much more than what Rome demanded and charged them for the right to collect the taxes. Therefore, it is not surprising that publicans were generally despised. But in the case of the Jews, this feeling was even more acute for a specific reason: because the publicans, even though they might be Jews, had to deal with Gentiles and so had to handle things considered unclean. As a consequence, good Jews did not have anything to do with publicans, and any Jews who did were simply considered sinners.

So this is the significant social and religious background against which the story of Levi — one of these publicans or tax collectors who were despised by the population at large as well as by the Pharisees and other religious people — takes place. Both Mark (2:13-17) and Matthew (9:13-17) refer to this episode, although in Matthew the name of the tax collector is not Levi but Matthew. The only thing that Luke adds to Mark's version of the story is that Levi, upon following Jesus, abandons everything (Luke 5:28). But this is not to be taken literally, for apparently Levi still has a home as well as the resources to hold a banquet. To this banquet he invites his friends as well as Jesus and his disciples. As is to be expected, many of Levi's friends are tax collectors like him, and those who are not are still considered particularly sinful because they associate with him. And, as is also to be expected, this leads to criticism on the part of the scribes and Pharisees, who are zealous about the Law; they believe that those who eat with unclean people become unclean themselves.

Jesus' response is well-known: "Those who are well have no need of a physician, but those who are sick; I have come to call not the righteous but sinners to repentance" (Luke 5:31-32).

In light of what has already been said about the great reversal, we see that Jesus' willingness to recline at the table with Levi and his friends is part of that great reversal, in which Pharisees and scribes are left behind tax collectors and sinners. So, here is one more instance of this Lukan theme which we have already discussed. But the fact that the same story appears also in Matthew and Mark reminds us that, although it is Luke who most stresses the theme of the great reversal, that theme appears throughout much of the Bible.

★   ★   ★

There are many other cases in which a meal provides an opportunity to announce the great reversal. One of these is the dinner at the home of Simon the Pharisee in Luke 7. Since this passage is similar to some in the other Gospels, what we often do is combine the stories to make a single story, when in truth the stories are different. In Matthew 26 and Mark 14, the banquet takes place at the home of "Simon the leper," not a word is said about the woman being sinful, and she anoints the head of Jesus with an expensive perfume. This is then followed by a discussion resulting from the feeling among the disciples that the perfume should have been sold and the money given to the poor. In John 12, the banquet takes place at the home of Martha and Mary; Mary anoints the feet of Jesus with an expensive perfume, and then dries them with her hair. This is followed by a discussion about what should have been done with the perfume that is similar to the discussions that appear in Matthew and Mark, although in this case it is Judas, and not the disciples in general, who criticizes Mary for being so wasteful. Since in

Matthew, Mark, and John the issue being discussed is whether the perfume ought to have been sold in order to benefit the poor, in all three of these Gospels Jesus declares that the woman has done well, for she has anointed him for his death.

The story that Luke tells is different. For example, in the parallel episodes in Matthew and Mark, Simon is a leper, but in Luke the host is a Pharisee. This seems to be so important to Luke that in the first verses of this story the man is known simply as "the Pharisee," and it is not until verse 40 that Jesus finally gives us his name. This helps us understand Luke's theology, for in the other Gospels Jesus does not eat with the Pharisees, but in Luke's Gospel he does so repeatedly.

If we then look more carefully at this subject of the Pharisees in Luke, we will note first of all that his Gospel is not as negative toward the Pharisees as is Matthew's. Certainly the Pharisees are not all that they ought to be. Some are hypocrites, and they are even looking for ways to accuse Jesus of blasphemy. But this is not true of all Pharisees.

Such is the case with Simon. We are so used to equating "Pharisee" with "hypocrite" that we assume that Simon also is one. And then we interpret what Luke says about him in the worst possible way. Thus we forget, for instance, that Simon's doubt about Jesus upon seeing him accepting the praise of the sinful woman has its positive side — as every doubt does. Simon is considering the possibility that Jesus may truly be a prophet, but the manner in which Jesus responds to the woman causes him to doubt that. Then follows the parable in which Jesus asks him who should be most grateful — one whose debt of fifty denarii has been forgiven, or one who has been forgiven a debt ten times as large. When Simon answers that the one who was forgiven the most should also be the most grateful, Jesus declares that he has judged the matter correctly. Then come Jesus' strong words of comparison between

83

Simon and the sinful woman: he did not even have the feet of Jesus washed, and she washed them with her tears; he did not give Jesus the expected welcome kiss, while she continued to kiss his feet; he did not give Jesus oil to anoint his head, while she anointed his feet with perfume. Jesus concludes by forgiving the sinful woman, saying, ". . . her sins, which were many, have been forgiven; hence she has shown great love. But the one to whom little is forgiven, loves little" (Luke 7:47). And so Jesus drives home the point of the parable. Certainly, these comparisons constitute strong criticism of Simon's attitude. But here, in contrast with other passages in Luke, and even more so with those in the other Gospels, Luke does not tell us that Simon rejected Jesus, or that from that point on he tried to catch him in an error, or that he began plotting his death. The episode that begins with doubt on Simon's part ends with doubts also among the other guests: "Who is this who even forgives sins?" (Luke 7:49). And we should note that even here Luke does not say that they were disturbed because Jesus claimed to be able to forgive sins. This we conclude by drawing from other passages, such as that of the bedridden man who is brought down through the roof. Here, at the meal in Simon's home, we are simply left wondering whether Simon and his guests believe or not.

At the beginning of this story, Luke tells us that a Pharisee invited Jesus to eat in his home, and that Jesus "took his place at the table" (Luke 7:36). A more exact translation would say that he reclined at the table, which would help us understand what is taking place. At such dinners, it was customary for people to recline on their left side, with their head toward the table and their feet away from it, and to eat with their right hand. This is why Luke tells us that the woman was behind Jesus, at his feet, so that she can reach his feet and wipe them with her hair. It is significant to note that in Luke's rendition of the story, there is no discussion about the value of the perfume, or whether it should have been sold. We draw all that from the other Gospels. In Luke, the stress is not on the value of the perfume or on what the woman did with it, but rather on the woman's profound humility and repentance as she washes the feet of Jesus with her tears, anoints them with perfume, and then dries them with her hair. Despite Luke's clear interest in the poor, in his Gospel this story leads not to a discussion about the poor or about what ought to have been done with the perfume, as in the other Gospels, but rather to a contrast between the Pharisee and the woman. As we have seen, in this case also, the meal becomes an opportunity to announce the great reversal one more time. This reversal is not only social and economic, but also religious and spiritual: the sinful woman is praised, while the religious Pharisee is criticized. This story about the meal in Simon's home is also a practical response to what precedes it in the same chapter. There Jesus says that when John the Baptist came preaching in the desert, all the people — "including the tax collectors" — listened to him and repented, while the Pharisees and the interpreters of the law did not do so. Jesus then goes on to affirm that those who rejected John the Baptist, saying "He has a demon," now reject him too, claiming that he is "a glutton and a drunkard, a friend of tax collectors and sinners!" (Luke 7:24-34).

Within this context, this meal with Simon the Pharisee may be seen as a response to these comments. What takes place at the dinner illustrates once again why the tax collectors and sinners are better companions at the table than the Pharisees. Yet the very fact that Luke does not say that the Pharisee and his guests rejected Jesus, but instead leaves the matter open, is a sign that the great reversal does not mean that the Pharisees are definitively and necessarily excluded from the reign of God. (It may also be worthwhile to note that something similar happens in the parable of the prodigal son, which never tells us whether, after his father talks to him, the elder son joins the feast. Also, something similar appears in the parable of the Good Samaritan, which ends when Jesus tells the scribe who is questioning him "Go and do likewise" [Luke 10:37]; we are not then told whether he did this or not.)

★   ★   ★

This is of utmost importance as we seek to interpret the Gospel of Luke for today, for the attitudes of most Pharisees are similar to those of most religious people today. As soon as we hear the word *Pharisee*, we decide that this refers to a hypocrite and an enemy of the gospel. Certainly there are passages in Luke (and many more in Matthew) that lead us to think that way, for Jesus himself calls some Pharisees "hypocrites." See, for instance, Luke 11:42-44, which records words of Jesus at the home of another Pharisee. But most Pharisees were not hypocrites; they were sincere people who made every effort to obey the Law in every particular circumstance. Jesus attacks them not because they were particularly bad, but because they were people who generally considered themselves to be better than the rest. In truth, many of the Pharisees of that time were much like us Christians today. We are so constantly preoccupied with doing this or that, or not doing this or that, that we forget that the two main commandments are commandments of love.

If the Pharisees, the most religious people of their time, were to be definitely excluded from the reign of God, what hope would there be for us religious people of today? Luke gives us heartening examples. By leaving open the question of whether or not Simon the Pharisee and his guests repented and accepted Jesus, Luke is leaving the door open so that we too who believe ourselves to be very religious and even better than others will still be able to enter the banquet. When we realize this, we see that Luke, while condemning the superficial and external religiosity of some Pharisees, also speaks of Pharisees who respond positively to Jesus' ministry and the call of the gospel. Thus, in Luke 5, in the story of the paralytic who is brought into the house through the roof, we see that those who are present are "Pharisees and doctors of the law" who at first are surprised that Jesus forgives the sins of the man, but who at the end of the story declare, "We have seen strange things today" (Luke 5:26). At some point after the meal in Luke 11 where Jesus speaks harshly against Pharisees and scribes, those who are present leave and begin plotting how to catch him in an error. But in Luke 13, when Jesus is in peril, Luke tells us that some Pharisees warn him: "Get away from here, for Herod wants to kill you" (Luke 13:31). This episode, which is not found in the other Gospels, is one more indication that Luke is not condemning all Pharisees in general. This encouraging viewpoint continues in the book of Acts. In Acts 5:33-39, we see that the Pharisee Gamaliel tries to stop those who are persecuting the apostles, thus playing a role similar to that of those who warned Jesus about Herod's intentions. Later, in Acts 15:5, we hear of Pharisees who have believed. But above all, it is important to remember that a good part of the book of Acts is devoted to the conversion and ministry of an apostle who near the end of that book still declares, "I am a Pharisee, a son of Pharisees" (Acts 23:6). The great reversal, while affirming that the Pharisees and those who are particularly religious have no advantage when it comes to the reign of God, also shows that even the strictest Pharisee may find the way of salvation.

In Luke 11, mentioned earlier in passing, Jesus is once again invited to dine at the home of a Pharisee whose name is not given. Jesus enters and immediately reclines to eat. The Pharisee wonders why Jesus did not wash before eating. At this point it is important to explain that this was not a matter of hygiene, as it is today when parents insist that children wash their hands before sitting at the dinner table. It was a matter of ritual, a matter of washing away all the uncleanness one might have come into contact with before coming to the table. Luke does not tell us if the Pharisee commented on the matter or if Jesus simply knew what he was thinking. In any case, from the consideration of washing before eating comes Jesus' diatribe with six woes ("Woe to you"), first against the Pharisees, and then against the lawyers. The first three are addressed to the Pharisees — the first, because they are so minutely conscientious about the tithe that they tend to leave aside justice and love of God; the second, because they seek to take the most important places in the synagogues, and to be greeted with respect in the city squares; and the third, because they are like unmarked graves over which people walk. Since a grave was considered unclean, this meant that in their supposed cleanness they were actually leading others astray into uncleanness. When one of the lawyers complains that he and his fellow lawyers are offended, Jesus addresses the next three woes to them, telling them, among other things, that when it comes to the knowledge God and of God's Law, they are like a dog in a manger: "For you have taken away the key of knowledge; you did not enter yourselves, and you hindered those who were entering" (Luke 11:52). This dinner at the home of an unnamed Pharisee is not mentioned in the other Gospels, although some of the things that Jesus says here about the Pharisees and the lawyers are certainly to be found in Matthew and Mark. What is different in Luke is that all of this takes place in a sort of symposium — a meal, as we noted, where people gather in order to discuss a theme. Luke thus depicts Jesus as reclining at a table with a group of Pharisees and lawyers who have invited him for some polite and edifying conversation, only to be surprised to hear words that they find offensive.

*　　　*　　　*

The next meal which Luke describes in some detail takes place in chapter 19, in the home of Zacchaeus. But before turning to it, and in order to understand its importance within the structure of the entire Gospel of Luke, we must take a moment to look at the parable of the great feast, which appears in chapter 14 — approximately in the middle between the dinner at the home of the unnamed Pharisee and the other dinner in the home of Zacchaeus the tax collector. In that parable Jesus speaks of a great feast to which a man invited many people — presumably his friends. But those initial invitees offer a series of excuses and will not attend the dinner. So the host orders his servant to find new guests: "Go out at once into the streets and lanes of the town and bring in the poor, the crippled, the blind, and the lame" (Luke 14:21). These people, whom most hosts would not even invite, will now share the special dinner that has been prepared. And then Jesus ends the parable with one more of those pronouncements that point to the great reversal: "I tell you, none of those who were invited will taste my dinner" (Luke 14:24).

If we begin from that parable and first look back to the dinner in chapter 11 and then look forward to the other dinner with Zacchaeus in chapter 19, we see that these two dinners are a joint confirmation of what Jesus says in the parable. In chapter 11, at the home of the Pharisee, Jesus condemns both the Pharisees and the lawyers — the most religious people in Israel, those who sought to fulfill the law in every detail, those who devoted themselves to the study of scripture. Now, in chapter 19, at the home of Zacchaeus, Jesus declares, "Today salvation has come to this house" (Luke 19:9). And he is saying this in the home of a tax collector, one of those whom religious people would consider unclean and unworthy sinners.

There are several points in the story of Zacchaeus that are worthy of note. The first is that, as was to be expected, the fact that Jesus enters a tax collector's house results in grumbling (or perhaps today we would say "gossiping"), not only among the Pharisees and lawyers, but also among the people in general. Luke tells us, "All who saw it began to grumble and said, 'He has gone to be the guest of one who is a sinner'" (Luke 19:7). This reminds us of the parable of the great feast, in which those who were invited and should have been present are outside, while those who would normally be outside are now inside, participating in the feast.

The second point to be noted is that Jesus invites himself to the home of Zacchaeus, while in the previous two dining situations with Pharisees, it was they who invited Jesus. This reminds us of the strange words in the parable, in which the host tells the servant not only to go and bring people from the street, but also to "compel [them] to come in" (Luke 14:23). Similarly, Jesus compels Zacchaeus to receive him in his home. It is Jesus who commands, who decides. In contrast, the Pharisees invite Jesus to dine with them, but they intend to continue being lords of their own households. But Jesus will not accept such lordship, and he dares to speak openly, even against his own hosts.

The third point to be noted is that, while in the cases of the Pharisees there is only a meal, in the case of Zacchaeus Jesus is to stay with him. When it is Jesus who invites — or who invites himself — the resulting relationship has a depth and a permanence that cannot take place when it is merely a dinner to which others invite and which they expect to control.

Finally, it is important to note that in the case of Zacchaeus, precisely because it is Jesus who invites and therefore who commands, the host changes radically. The dinners with the Pharisees are like symposia, occasions to converse and discuss a subject. But the visit of Jesus to Zacchaeus's house produces a profound change in his host: "Look, half of my possessions, Lord, I will give to the poor; and if I have defrauded anyone of anything, I will pay back four times as much" (Luke 19:8).

To summarize, then: we have stories of four meals: the first takes place at the home of Levi, a tax collector; the second and third occur in the homes of Pharisees; and the fourth takes place once again in the home of a tax collector — in this case, Zacchaeus. In the middle of them, between the second and the third, we have the parable of the great feast, which explains much of what happens in the stories of the four meals that surround it.

*　　*　　*

In the Gospel of Luke there are still two other important meals that deserve particular consideration: the Last Supper before Jesus' crucifixion, and the meal at Emmaus after Jesus' resurrection. These two meals and their significance are such that they deserve separate consideration. Therefore, rather than discussing them in this chapter, we will use them as a point of departure for the subject of the next chapter: worship in Luke's theology.

Before finishing this chapter, however, it is important to remember that, even though we have discussed quite a few meals of which Jesus partook, this does not exhaust the theme of food in Luke's theology and writings. Among other passages that could be discussed are the story in Luke 6 about collecting wheat to eat on the Sabbath; the story in chapter 9 about the feeding of the five thousand; and the parable in chapter 16 about the rich man and Lazarus. These passages, together with those others that we have discussed in more detail, show the importance of food in Luke's theology, and the manner in which meals themselves are occasions to speak both of the great reversal and of the hope of salvation. Thus in Luke's writings, as throughout Scripture, one of the most common images used to refer to the coming of God's reign is a great banquet. But in Luke, banquets and other references to food serve to clarify the nature of that final feast, who will sit at it, and who, in spite of having been invited, will be absent.

SEVEN

Luke and Worship

Then their eyes were opened, and they recognized him.
Luke 24:31

TOO OFTEN THE THEME of worship is excluded or set aside from theological matters, when in fact theology and praise, doctrine and worship, are so interwoven that if we separate them, they both lose much of their significance and value. Even though, when we study and discuss the history of Christian thought or of Christian doctrines, we imagine that that they are the result of theological speculation or of the training of the faithful, the truth is that doctrine and theology are shaped and communicated in worship.

Historians refer to this as the principle of *lex orandi est lex credendi*, which actually means that the rule of worship becomes the rule of faith, that doctrine is born in worship, and what defines the church, giving it unity and coherence, is its worship much more than its doctrines.

And, if it is true that in order to understand any theology, we must take into account the worship context in which it is formed, we should note that this is consistently emphasized in Luke's writings, which constantly point to worship. The Gospel of Luke begins with the temple, with the vision of Zechariah when he is serving in the sanctuary. Then comes the story of the presentation of Jesus in the temple, which appears only in Luke. Of all the Evangelists, only Luke tells us that the family of Jesus went annually to worship in the temple, and only he records the visit of Jesus to the temple when he was twelve years old. Only Luke sets an important part of the ministry of Jesus in the context of a journey from Galilee to Jerusalem and its temple. And, in its very last verse, the Third Gospel takes us back to the place where the whole story began by declaring that, after the Resurrection, Jesus' disciples "were continually in the temple blessing God" (Luke 24:53).

Furthermore, it is Luke who includes in the very first few chapters of his Gospel four hymns that to this day have an important role in the worship of many churches: first, the song of Mary ("My soul magnifies the Lord. . . ."); second, the prophecy of Zechariah ("Blessed be the Lord God of Israel. . . ."); third, the brief canticle of the angels ("Glory to God in the highest heaven. . . ."); and fourth, the praise of Simeon ("Master, now you are dismissing your servant in peace. . . ."). These four hymns are usually known by their first words in Latin: the Magnificat, the Benedictus, the Gloria, and the Nunc dimittis. And they have had an important place in the worship of the church over the centuries. Furthermore, it has been suggested that these hymns were already in use in the church when Luke wrote his Gospel, and that it was from Christian worship that Luke took them. In any case, there is no doubt that from the very beginning to this day, there has been a close relationship between the worship of the church and the writings of Luke.

*   *   *

This is why, as we seek to understand Luke's theology, we have to look at the context of worship in which it was formed, and how that theology in turn impacted the worship of the church. Although there are no documents that tell us exactly what worship was like in the ancient church, there are at least two affirmations that may be made with certainty. The first is that the center of worship was communion. This may be seen in the descriptions of the life of the church in Acts 2, where Luke tells us that "Day by day, as they spent much time together in the temple, *they broke bread* at home and ate their food with glad and generous hearts, praising God . . ." (Acts 2:46-47; my italics). Much later, in chapter 20, Luke tells us what happened in Troas "on the first day of the week, *when we met to break bread*" (Acts 20:7; my italics). This is confirmed in the epistles, particularly Paul's First Letter to the Corinthians, where he not only repeats the story of the institution of the Lord's Supper, but also spends much time trying to instruct the believers in Corinth about how they are to behave in that celebration. Thus, the first thing we can affirm about worship in the early church is that it was centered in the breaking of bread — that is, in the Lord's Supper or communion.

Second, we can also affirm that much of the worship service consisted of scripture reading. Although there are no specific data from the first century, there is ample proof that in the second century the service of worship had two parts: the "service of the Word" and "the service of the Table." The latter was communion. But before communion was celebrated, there was the service of the Word. In order to understand the importance of that service, we must remember that this was long before the invention of the printing press, and that both papyrus and parchment were rather expensive. Therefore, there would be very few believers who had in their homes even one of the books of the Bible. The same was true among Jewish believers, among whom very few had scripture at home other than the verses written on their doorposts or worn on their foreheads in the way that Deuteronomy 11:18 commanded. So it was in the synagogue that Jews gathered in order to hear the reading and interpretation of scripture. Likewise, Christians gathered before the service of the Table so that in the service of the Word they could hear the reading and exposition of scripture that they could not read at home. From the very first years, the scriptures read were those of Israel — what today we call the Old Testament. But soon it became customary in some churches to read letters such as those by Paul. These letters, written to a congregation as a whole, would be read out loud to the congregation when they were received. After this reading, it is most likely that portions of the letters were used to try to interpret both what was said in the Old Testament and the experience of Christians at the time. They would also be shared with other churches that requested that copies be made for them. The same was true of the Gospels, which were also read in the service of the Word in preparation for the service of the Table. Therefore, when we read, for example, the epistles of Paul, we should remember that Paul was writing so that his epistles could be read in the service of the Word, when the gathered faithful were preparing for the service of the Table. And there is no doubt that the book of Revelation and the Gospel of John were written for the same purpose.

The first part of worship, the service of the Word, was a period of instruction in which scripture was taught and interpreted while keeping in mind the two central acts of Christian worship, baptism and communion. For those who were not yet baptized, the service of the Word was part of their instruction and preparation for their baptism. For those who were already baptized, it was at once a remembrance of their baptism and their preparation for the service of the Table, in which only the baptized could participate; the rest of the congregation was dismissed at the end of the service of the Word.

It is within this context that we are to understand Luke's many references to baptism. All the Gospels speak of the work of Jesus as a baptism more powerful than John's: baptism with the Holy Spirit. Matthew ends with the commission of the disciples to go and baptize. Luke continues his work with a second book in which he tells how this took place, and in which there are many references to baptism, in water as well as in the Spirit. Thus, from the beginning of Acts we are told that multitudes were baptized during Pentecost, that many Samaritans and the Ethiopian eunuch were baptized by Philip, that Cornelius and his household were also baptized, and so on. Therefore, even though Luke does not tell us how baptism was administered, there is no doubt that baptism and its meaning were constantly in the background of his entire work, particularly in Acts.

Since the Gospels were read in the service of the Word, in preparation for the breaking of bread, those passages referring to the last supper of the Lord with his disciples soon became part of the service of the Table. Therefore, we should not be surprised that in 1 Corinthians 11, when discussing the Lord's Supper, Paul tells the story of that last meal before Jesus' crucifixion. For the same reason, passages having to do with food and drink became especially important for the worship of the church. In the case of Luke, which was written when there were already Gospels being read in the congregation, one may ask to what extent the possible use of what he was writing influenced his work. Furthermore, it is quite probable that Luke's emphasis on food — like John's emphasis on both food and drink — may be due to his expectation that his book would be read to the entire congregation in the service of the Word for the instruction of all believers, but particularly in preparation for the service of the Table or Lord's Supper.

In the previous chapter, while discussing the subject of Luke and food, we left aside two of the most important meals mentioned in his Gospel: the Last Supper and the breaking of bread in Emmaus. These two deserve particular attention, for they are very important to understand the theology of Luke in the context of worship within which and for which Luke was writing.

*   *   *

It is significant that among the Four Gospels, the two that include a supper of the Lord after his resurrection are Luke and John — precisely the last two that were written, and therefore the two that are more likely to have been written with a view to their use in the service of the Word. If we then read the Gospel of Luke thinking about how those early Christians in the first century and early second century would have read it, we shall find in it meanings that we would otherwise overlook. Many examples could be quoted to show this, but a few will suffice.

First, when those early Christians heard Mary praise God because "he has filled the hungry with good things" (Luke 1:53), this would have built bridges between their own condition and the meal they were about to celebrate. As far as we know, among those Christians there were, as Paul says, not many who were wise by human standards, or powerful or of noble birth. They were not people with an overabundance of goods, or even of food. Many of them would literally be hungry. But now Mary announced to them a new order, a new reality, a new reign in which God would fill the hungry with good things. Out there, in the world, there might be rich people who believed that they were happy, but in truth they were hungry. But in this community of faith, where believers were to celebrate in the coming meal, they had the true bread of life eternal, the true foretaste of the reign of God. And at this point it may be important to add that in the early church, that was exactly what happened in communion, a meal to which everyone brought what they could, and in which by means of sharing even the hungry were satisfied. (This explains why Paul was so angry when he learned that in Corinth there were some who overate at the table of the Lord, which meant that others were still hungry.)

A second example is found in Luke 6. There we find the story of the disciples gathering wheat on the Sabbath, and some Pharisees criticizing them. Jesus responds by reminding the Pharisees that even David, when he and those who were with him were hungry, took consecrated bread that they should not have been allowed to eat; Jesus then goes on to declare that "the Son of Man is Lord of the sabbath" (Luke 6:5). In a way, this episode is parallel to many others in which Jesus heals someone on the Sabbath, and the lawyers and Pharisees call him to account. In those passages as well as in this one, the issue is whether the Law of God is above human need and above the practice of love. At this point it is important to make clear that the law of the Sabbath is neither wrong nor evil. It has been given by God. Jesus does not say that his disciples ought to pay no attention to it. What he does say is that laws given by God have been given out of love, and are not to be employed to keep the ill in pain, or keep the hungry unsatisfied.

Imagine a congregation around the year 90 gathered on a Sunday, perhaps at four or five in the morning, in order to participate first in the service of the Word and then in the service of the Table. In the service of the Word, they hear these words from the Gospel of Luke. And what they are celebrating is a consequence of what Jesus says here: that he, Jesus, the Lord of the Sabbath, provides food for his disciples even though the social order and the laws — including good laws — would seek to impede that. This was precisely what was happening in the Roman Empire. To this day, that Empire is justly recognized for the thoroughness of its laws. Without those laws, chaos would have reigned, so they were good and necessary laws. But, as in every human society, there were those who employed those laws in order to hoard power and food, denying them to the rest of the population. In the face of that reality, Christians knew that there, in that supper that they were about to celebrate, the Lord of the Sabbath and of all laws provided for them the food of eternity — just as before, walking in the fields, he provided food for his disciples. It is significant that in the same chapter, a few verses later, Jesus himself says, "Blessed are you who are hungry now, for you will be filled" (Luke 6:21).

The third example comes from the parable of the prodigal son. What most draws our attention today when we hear this parable is the love and mercy of the father, and his joy at the return of the son that was lost. But if we were about to celebrate a meal, as were those Christians who would read that story at some point around the year 90, we would also note that all of the story leads to a great banquet. The father not only receives his son, but also invites people to a special dinner. The forgiveness and the grace of God that those early Christians experienced were expressed in a meal, just as in the case of the prodigal son and the merciful father. But those Christians also knew that if they did not come to the Father in repentance, if they were to come claiming their rights, their obedience, or their holiness, they would be like that other son, who was unable to accept the joy of his father at the return of the lost son, and therefore excluded himself both from that joy and possibly from the meal prepared to celebrate it.

*   *   *

But, obviously, the main passage in the entire Gospel of Luke on this subject of eating and its relationship to communion is Luke 22, where we are told of the institution of the Supper itself in a paschal dinner of Jesus with his disciples. The passage is well-known, and there is no need to repeat it here. But we do need to stop and consider a dimension that we frequently miss: the eschatological projection of the Supper. In Luke as well as in Matthew and Mark, Jesus tells his disciples that he "will not drink of the fruit of the vine until the kingdom of God comes" (Luke 22:18; Matt. 26:29; Mark 14:25). But in Luke, Jesus says this not only about the wine but also about the food: "I will not eat it until it is fulfilled in the kingdom of God" (Luke 22:16). In all three Synoptic Gospels, the Last Supper has an eschatological dimension, for Jesus will not drink again with his disciples until he does so in the reign of God. But in Luke this dimension is stressed by being mentioned twice. The Last Supper points to the future, to the feast of the wedding of the Lamb, to the time when "people will come from the east and west, from north and south, and will eat in the kingdom of God" (Luke 13:29).

In Luke, Jesus not only says that he will eat again with his disciples in the reign of God, but also says that in that eschatological banquet, one will see the fulfillment of the supper he now celebrates with his disciples in the upper room: "I will not eat it until it is *fulfilled* in the kingdom of God" (my emphasis). The verb that Jesus employs here, *pleroo*, means "to fulfill, to complete, to bring to fruition." Therefore, what Jesus is telling us in Luke is that this supper, no matter whether we consider it "the Last," is also in a way the first, the beginning that will come to fruition only in the final day.

Sadly, we have often lost that eschatological dimension of the Lord's Supper. We take the words "Do this in remembrance of me" (1 Cor. 11:24) and we make them the center of our interpretation of communion, thus thinking that what we are to do when we partake of it is to center our thoughts on the crucified Jesus and on his death for us. What we forget is that these words appear only in First Corinthians and in Luke (22:19), but not in any of the other Gospels. This does not mean that they are not true and important. But if they were the central theme of the Lord's Supper, it would be difficult to understand why the other Evangelists do not mention them. Therefore, rather than understanding communion essentially on the basis of those words, we ought to try to understand it in light of what all the Evangelists tell us about the Supper. And part of what they tell us is that the Supper has an eschatological dimension, that it points to the future. Furthermore, Luke clearly says that the promise of the Supper itself is fulfilled only in that eschatological future.

At this point it might be wise to digress for a moment and consider again the words of Jesus in First Corinthians and Luke: "Do this in remembrance of me." What is here translated as "memory" is the word *anamnesis*, which certainly has the meaning of "memory," but refers to more than the past. Actually, even in common usage we use the notion of remembering to refer to more than the past. We say "Remember where you're coming from," but we also say "Remember where you are" and "Remember where you're going" — referring to the present and the future. What Jesus tells his disciples in First Corinthians is that they are to bring him to mind. This means remembering the past (his crucifixion and resurrection), the present (his presence in the church by virtue of the Holy Spirit), and the future (the day in which he is to eat with us in the reign of God). Thus, doing this "in remembrance of" him is to remember the past, the present, and the future.

As we can see, what has just been said regarding the *anamnesis* fits perfectly with the Lukan eschatological dimension of communion. The Lord's Supper is not only a remembrance of the past, but also the occasion to bring to mind the presence of Jesus in the church and above all to remember that the Supper in itself is somehow incomplete, for it has not yet been fulfilled in the reign of God.

Then there is the meal appearing only in Luke, in which Jesus, following his resurrection, sits down to eat with two of his disciples in Emmaus. Luke tells us about this event in chapter 24 of his Gospel. Although this story is well-known, when we look at it and take into account the theme of worship, and specifically of communion, the use of four verbs in verse 30 stands out: "When he was at the table with them, he *took* bread, *blessed* and *broke* it, and *gave* it to them" (my emphasis). Three of these verbs appear in the story of the Last Supper: "He took a loaf of bread, and when he had *given thanks*, he *broke* it and *gave* it to them" (Luke 22:19; my emphasis). The second verb is practically the same in both stories: in one story we are told he "blessed," and in the other that he "gave thanks." Given these similarities, there is no doubt that the supper at Emmaus is connected with the Lord's Supper. The Emmaus meal marks the first time that some of Jesus' disciples break bread with the resurrected Lord. What first appears to be a common, everyday meal becomes the Lord's Supper in this act of taking bread and blessing it, breaking it, and giving it.

This takes us to the second important point in the story of Emmaus, which is what these two disciples said to the others upon returning to Jerusalem: "they told . . . how he had been made known to them in the breaking of the bread" (Luke 24:35). For those believers that we have been imagining, gathered to worship the Lord on a Sunday morning at some point around the year 90, when this story was read in the service of the Word, in preparation for communion, such references must have been obvious: Jesus broke bread with his disciples, and in that very act he made himself known to them. The same has been the understanding of believers through the ages: that when we *take* this bread, *bless* it, *break* it, and *give* it, in these very acts the Lord is made known to us. In the Supper, at the same time that we remember the return of the Lord, that very Lord comes to share the table with his disciples. In that moment, eschatology is not only a matter of the future but becomes also a present reality — a reality for this present in which we live as we remember the past and anticipate the future.

★   ★   ★

Luke continues dealing with the theme of communion in his second book, Acts. Some passages that refer to the breaking of the bread have already been quoted. The first of them, in Acts 2, tells us that after breaking the bread, the believers "ate their food with glad and generous hearts" (Acts 2:46). This may well surprise us, for many of us have grown up with a view of communion that has little to celebrate. We have been taught that what we ought to do in communion is to think about the sufferings and death of Christ, and about our sin, which made such a horrible death necessary. Communion then becomes an occasion for us to meditate on our sin and on the sufferings of Christ, and thereby be led to repentance.

That is why it might seem strange to us that in the early church, and for many centuries thereafter, communion was not an opportunity for sadness and grieving, but rather a matter of joy. This is why Luke says that those early Christians broke their bread joyfully. This is why even today we speak of "celebrating" communion. Celebrations are joyful occasions of gratitude rather than repentance. They are occasions of hope rather than grieving. In the early church, communion was a time of joy, gratitude, and hope.

All of this is connected with what has just been said about what is "remembered" in communion. If what we remember is only the cross of Christ and our sin requiring it, communion is certainly a time of mourning and repentance. But if what we remember is above all the victory of Christ both in his resurrection and in the establishment of the reign of God, if what we remember is his presence among us by the work of the Spirit, then communion is a time of joy, gratitude, and hope.

This is related to the day of the week on which the ancient church gathered to celebrate communion. The phrase "the first day of the week" appears twice in Luke. The first time is in the Gospel, when Luke tells us that on the first day of the week, very early in the morning, the women went to the tomb (Luke 24:1). The second time is in Acts, when the disciples are gathered with Paul in Troas on the first day of the week (Acts 20:7). The church

gathered to break bread on the first day of the week because that
was the day of the resurrection of Jesus. Friday was a day of fasting
and mourning, for it was the day of the crucifixion. Saturday was
a time for reflection and for rest for those who were able to rest —
for many of the earliest Christians were slaves or other people who
could not simply rest at whatever time they chose. But, since the
next day the church would gather in order to celebrate communion,
it soon became common to call Saturday "the day of preparation,"
and this is its name in several ancient texts.

In ancient times, as today, time was measured in cycles. The
most important of these was the week. In Israel, within the week
the most important day was the Sabbath — to the point that the
other days were simply called "the first day after the Sabbath," "the
second day after the Sabbath," "two days before the Sabbath," and
so on. Several feasts and important dates were also based on the
cycle of a week. Thus, for instance, "a week of weeks" — that is,
forty-nine days — after Passover came the day of Pentecost. And
there were also weeks of years and weeks of weeks of years, so that
after forty-nine years there was to be a year of jubilee.

Thus, in cycles of seven and seven and seven more, time went
on. After each Saturday came the first day of the week, which in
its turn would leave its place to the second, and so on until the
next Sabbath, which would again be followed by the first day of
the week, and so on in an unending cycle. Ah, but there is more.
There was in the early church a tradition about the "eighth day."
This is the way of referring to the final day, to the consummation
of creation and the final victory of the Lord. So on a certain day,
upon awakening after the night of the Sabbath, it will dawn on us
that the cycle is now complete! That instead of the first day of the
week, it is now the eighth! This is a day that comes only once, for it
is the final day, the day towards which are moving all other days, all
other weeks, all the weeks of weeks of years! In the ancient church,

what had happened on that first day of the week when the women went to the tomb and found it empty was the dawning of the eighth day. From then on, believers have lived both within the apparently unending cycles of history and in the final day, the reign of God, for by reason of their union with Christ they have a foretaste of that reign. There is still a "first day," a "second day," and so on. But now, by virtue of that day of the week on which the women found the tomb empty, we are able to live in the eighth day, in the new creation. (This is the reason why to this day many baptistries and baptismal fonts are octagonal.)

This brings us back to the eschatological dimensions of communion. When Christians gathered to break bread in memory of Jesus, what they remembered were two closely linked events: on the one hand, a past event, the resurrection and victory of Jesus; and on the other hand, a future event, his final victory. Both are events leading to joy, and that is why those early Christians broke bread "with glad and generous hearts."

There is also a third event that makes the first day of the week particularly important. In one of the creation stories in Genesis, we are told that God made the world in six days and rested on the seventh — that is, the Sabbath. This means that God began creating the world six days before the Sabbath, or on the first day of the week. Therefore, the first day of the week on which the women went to the tomb is connected with the first day of all creation as well as with the eighth day.

*　　　*　　　*

There is another passage in Acts that has clear connections with communion — the story of Paul and the storm at sea in Acts 27:13-44. (This happens immediately before the shipwreck.) For two weeks Paul and the others onboard had been struggling against the wind and the waves. The situation was so desperate that the sailors had plotted to abandon ship and leave behind the soldiers as well as Paul and his fellow prisoners so that they would all sink with the ship. Nobody even took time to eat. In the midst of that despair, Paul spoke a word of hope: "I urge you to take some food, for it will help you survive; for none of you will lose a hair from your heads" (Acts 27:34). And Luke then continues his story, declaring that after Paul had said this, "he took bread, and giving thanks to God in the presence of all, he broke it and began to eat" (Acts 27:35). Note the verbs that appear here: "he *took* bread, and *giving thanks* . . . , he *broke* it and *began to eat*." The first three are the same verbs that appear repeatedly in the various references to communion mentioned before. The verb that is lacking is "gave" in the sense of sharing, for in this case Paul eats by himself rather than giving of the bread to the soldiers and sailors. The connotation of a communion service is undeniable. The only difference is that here, since those who are with him are not believers, Paul does not give them the bread. Therefore, it is possible to understand this episode as a communion service in the presence of the unbelieving soldiers and sailors. And it is particularly interesting to note that once Paul had given them hope by eating before them, "all of them were encouraged and took food for themselves" (Acts 27:36).

As this passage suggests, worship, and particularly communion, is an activity of the church; but it must also be hope for the world. This is why in First Corinthians Paul declares that "as often as you eat this bread and drink the cup, you proclaim the Lord's death until he comes" (1 Cor. 11:26). Communion is an announcement, a proclamation to the world around us. In the story of the storm at sea in Acts, the sailors and soldiers despaired and believed that they were already lost. But by eating before them, Paul opened a future for them, a hope. Paul invited those who were traveling with him, including his guards, to eat because it would help them survive.

All of this means that when the church worships, when the church breaks bread together, that worship and that breaking of bread, even though they may take place within the walls of the church building, are an announcement to the entire world of the death and resurrection of the Lord, as well as of his coming reign. In Paul's case, in a ship about to be destroyed, and in ours, in a world that sinks into despair, part of the task of believers is to give hope. The ship may be about to be wrecked, and the world may be in parallel straits, but there is still hope, for God is still Lord of the oceans and of history. Paul took bread, blessed it, broke it, and ate. But in that very action he also invited the soldiers and sailors to eat, and thus to regain hope. In Luke's theology, worship is also an announcement to all of humanity — an announcement of love, justice, peace, and hope.

Thus, this work in two books, which begins by telling Theophilus that what he will read is grafted into the entire history of humanity, ends also by showing him that it is precisely by reason of that story of Jesus and of the Spirit that there is still a hope to be proclaimed to all humankind. At the beginning of the narrative, Caesar, without even knowing it, causes Jesus to be born in Bethlehem. At the end of the narrative, Paul is about to appear before Caesar, who does not know that in the witness and faith of this prisoner are the hope and future not only of his empire, but of the entire universe.

Earlier we saw that we are living in a time when we are losing the sense of the true value of food — of food not only as nutrition for the body, but as the center of a social and even a religious activity. The popularity of fast food and fast consumption undermine both healthy eating and eating as a social occasion, as a humanizing activity — the notion of a meal as a symposium. But this is simply a symptom of a time when we seem to have lost the sense of both a past and a future, and therefore humanity finds itself in a stormy sea without an anchor and without hope. In its worship, in this eating together that is communion, the church has the opportunity and the duty to give the world a glimpse of a life between the past of what God has done and the future of what God has promised to do; between the past of the crucifixion and resurrection of the Lord, and the future of his return and his reign. When the church gathers to break bread and drink wine in remembrance of its Lord, it does this bringing to mind the cross and the resurrection, bringing to mind the One who is to come, and bringing to mind that he is already with us, for the One who is to come is the Risen One whom we already know and who is already in our present.

EIGHT

Luke and the Holy Spirit

He will be filled with the Holy Spirit.

Luke 1:15

THERE IS NO DOUBT that Luke gives great importance to the
person and work of the Holy Spirit. In the Gospel of Mark there
are only about six references to the Holy Spirit. In Matthew, there
are only about twelve. There are sixteen in the Third Gospel. But it
is above all in Acts that Luke stresses the theme of the Holy Spirit,
for there are almost sixty references to it there. (The reason for
speaking in terms of approximate numbers is that in some cases it
is not clear whether Mark and Matthew are referring to the "Spirit"
— that is, to the Holy Spirit — or to the "spirit" — that is, to the
human spirit.)

But the importance of the Spirit for Luke is not limited to the
number of his references. It is even more apparent in the passages
of his Gospel that are typically Lukan, as well as in his use of expressions that have come to be part of the universal inheritance of
the entire church, and in the very structure of his books.

*   *   *

Let us look first at some of those passages that are typically Lukan. By this I mean those that do not have an exact parallel in the
other Gospels. But we should not leave aside those that do have

parallels, and should at least be mentioned. First of all, in Luke 3:16 we have the announcement by John the Baptist that the one coming after him will baptize "with the Holy Spirit and fire," words that appear also in Matthew and Mark, although the latter does not mention fire. Likewise, the descent of the Spirit upon Jesus at his baptism is found in all four Gospels. In the three Synoptics, in their narrative about Jesus in the desert, we find that the Spirit is present and active in the story. But if we study carefully the Greek text of this narrative, we see that in Matthew, Jesus was "taken" by the Spirit to the desert, in Mark he was "impelled" or "thrown" by the Spirit into the desert, and in Luke he "went" and "was" in the desert "in the Spirit." At the end of the story, the only Gospel writer saying that Jesus returned to Galilee "filled with the power of the Spirit" is Luke (Luke 4:14). After this episode, the Spirit does not appear again in Matthew until chapter 10, when — in a passage that has parallels in Mark 13 and Luke 12 — Jesus tells his disciples that when they are called to witness before the courts, it will be the Spirit who will speak through them. In addition, the reference to the sin against the Spirit in Matthew 12 has its parallels in Mark 3 and Luke 12. And the same is true of the reference to the Spirit speaking through David in Psalm 110, which may be found in Matthew 22, Mark 12, and Luke 20.

There are only two passages in Matthew referring to the Spirit that have no parallel in Luke. One of them is the quotation from Isaiah in Matthew 12:18-21. The other appears in the same chapter, when Jesus says that "if it is by the Spirit of God that I cast out demons, then the kingdom of God has come to you" (Matt. 12:28). In this particular case, Luke says, ". . . if it is by the finger of God that I cast out the demons, then . . ." (Luke 11:20). As for Mark, there is not a single reference to the Holy Spirit in that Gospel that does not appear also in Luke.

In contrast, there are numerous passages in Luke in which he speaks about the Holy Spirit, and which have no exact parallel in the other Gospels. It will be instructive to look at some of them.

The Holy Spirit has an important place in the stories of Jesus' birth and his early years that appear only in Luke. As early as chapter 1, Zechariah is promised that his son "even before his birth . . . will be filled with the Holy Spirit" (Luke 1:15). Then, in the Annunciation, the angel Gabriel says to Mary, "The Holy Spirit will come upon you, and the power of the Most High will overshadow you" (Luke 1:35). A few verses later, Luke tells us that when John leapt in his mother's womb, she "was filled with the Holy Spirit and exclaimed with a loud cry . . ." (Luke 1:41-42). And a few sentences thereafter, in verse 67, Luke says that when John was born, Zechariah "was filled with the Holy Spirit and spoke this prophecy. . . ." In chapter 2, when Jesus is presented in the temple, Luke says of Simeon that "the Holy Spirit rested on him," and that "it had been revealed to him by the Holy Spirit that he would not see death before he had seen the Lord's Messiah" (Luke 2:25-27).

As already mentioned, in chapter 4, after the Spirit accompanies him in the desert, Jesus returns to Galilee "filled with the power of the Spirit." Then comes the episode at the synagogue in Nazareth, where Jesus reads a passage that begins "The Spirit of the Lord is upon me . . ." (Luke 4:18). Further on, in chapter 10, when the seventy return from their mission, Jesus rejoices in the Spirit (Luke 10:21). In chapter 11, after giving his disciples a model for prayer, he asks them questions by way of illustration: "Is there anyone among you who, if your child asks for a fish, will give a snake instead of a fish? Or if the child asks for an egg, will give a scorpion? If you, then, who are evil, know how to give good gifts to your children, how much more will the heavenly Father give the Holy Spirit to those who ask him!" (Luke 11:11-13). This passage contrasts with the parallel in Matthew 7:11, where what Jesus promises is that the Father will give "good things" to those who ask.

★ ★ ★

But in order to understand the theme of the Holy Spirit in Luke's writings, it is not enough for us simply to look at those passages that may be called uniquely Lukan; we also have to look at the terminology that Luke employs in his two books to refer to the Holy Spirit. Some of that terminology has become so common among us that we do not realize that it is almost exclusively Lukan. The clearest example of this is the very phrase "filled with the Holy Spirit," which rarely appears in the Bible anywhere except in Luke's two writings. The two other places that it does appear are Micah 3:8, when the prophet says that he is "filled with power, with the spirit of the LORD," and Ephesians 3:19, where the writer prays that his readers will be "filled with all the fullness of God." In Luke's two books this phrase appears twelve times — four times in the Gospel (in the instances just described), and eight times in Acts. On the day of Pentecost, all were "filled with the Holy Spirit" (Acts 2:4), and two chapters later, Peter addresses the Jewish council "filled with the Holy Spirit" (Acts 4:8). In chapter 6, one of the requisites for the seven who are to be named to serve at the tables is that they be "full of the Spirit" (Acts 6:3), and the same phrase is applied two other times to Stephen, one of those seven (Acts 6:5; Acts 7:55). Ananias promises Paul that he will recover his sight and that he will be "filled with the Holy Spirit" (Acts 9:17). Luke tells us that Barnabas was "a good man, full of the Holy Spirit and of faith" (Acts 11:24). And when Paul chastises the magician Elymas in Cyprus, he does this "filled with the Holy Spirit" (Acts 13:9).

In the entire New Testament, only Luke uses the verb "to fill" to refer to what happens to a person. For instance, in Nazareth "all in the synagogue were filled with rage" when they heard Jesus speak (Luke 4:28). In Cyprus, Paul tells Elymas that he is "full of all deceit and villainy" (Acts 13:10). And after leaving Antioch of Pisidia, the disciples were "filled with joy and with the Holy Spirit" (Acts 13:52). In all of these cases, being "filled" with something refers not to an interior attitude, but actually to an emotional or spiritual fullness that overflows outwardly. Whoever is filled with rage acts accordingly. Whoever is filled with deceit acts deceitfully. Likewise, being filled with the Holy Spirit is not an interior condition but is rather a spiritual reality that overflows outwardly. And just as being full of rage involves the whole person, so being full of the Holy Spirit involves the whole person, and is manifested outwardly in attitudes of goodness, wisdom, and joy.

Another typically Lukan image is the pouring out of the Spirit, which appears three times in the story of Pentecost (Acts 2:17, 18, 33), and later in the case of Cornelius and the other Gentiles with him (Acts 10:45). This image is parallel to the phrase about how Jesus will baptize — "with the Holy Spirit and fire" — in Luke 3:16, which does have parallels in the other Gospels: Matthew uses the same image, while Mark and John refer only to the promise by John the Baptist that another will come baptizing in the Holy Spirit. In Acts 1:5, Jesus declares that this promise is about to be fulfilled: "You will be baptized with the Holy Spirit not many days from now." Later, in Acts 11:16, Peter employs the same phrase in order to interpret what has happened to Cornelius.

Finally, it may be useful to point out that, although in all four Gospels we are told that upon the baptism of Jesus the Spirit descended upon him, the references to the Spirit "falling" on someone are typically Lukan.

Since all of these phrases are commonly used today among Christians of many different traditions, it is clear that Luke's contribution to the Christian doctrine of the Spirit is unparalleled in the New Testament.

*　　*　　*

Furthermore, this emphasis is not limited to isolated passages but may be seen also in the overall structure of Luke's works. Near the beginning of each of his two books, Luke quotes from a prophet, and in a way that quotation is an announcement of what will come in the rest of the book. In the Gospel, that quotation is the passage from Isaiah that Jesus reads in the synagogue, and which begins with the words "The Spirit of the Lord is upon me" (Luke 4:18). In Acts, the quotation comes from Joel and is placed in the mouth of Peter: "In the last days it will be, God declares, that I will pour out my Spirit upon all flesh" (Acts 2:17). Each of these two quotations outlines the program for God's action: in the Gospel, for God's action through Jesus; and in Acts, for God's action in the church. In the Gospel, by the power of the Spirit, Jesus will bring good news to the poor and announce release to the captives and recovery of sight to the blind. In Acts, the Spirit will be poured out on men and women, young and old, and even on Gentiles.

These two narratives are so closely bound together that one may well say that in the first of the two books we see the Spirit acting through Jesus, and in the second we see Jesus acting through the Spirit in the church. Luke addresses these two books to Theophilus. At the beginning of the second book, he tells him, "In the first book, Theophilus, I wrote about all that Jesus did and taught from the beginning until the day when he was taken up to heaven, after giving instructions through the Holy Spirit to the apostles whom he had chosen" (Acts 1:1-2). It is also possible to translate what Luke says this way: These are the things that Jesus began to teach and began to do until he was "taken up to heaven." But these things do not end with the first book; rather, they continue now, but take place through the Spirit.

Although we usually call Luke's second book "The Acts of the Apostles," in truth the book is not about the apostles, but rather about the Holy Spirit. Although early in the book the names of the Twelve are given, most of them soon disappear from the story. In the first chapters we are told more about Peter and John. But after chapter 4, John appears again only in chapter 8. Even Peter disappears after chapter 15, where he is part of the so-called Council at Jerusalem. Barnabas, whom Luke call an apostle even though he is not one of the Twelve (Acts 14:14), also disappears after chapter 15. Philip, one of the Seven, is named in chapter 6 and is the central figure in chapter 8, but is not mentioned again until chapter 21. Timothy is first mentioned in chapter 16, comes in and out of the scene until chapter 20, and after that is not mentioned again. Even in the case of Paul, who appears for the first time in chapter 7 and soon seems to become the protagonist of the story, Luke does not tell us what became of him. At the end of the book we learn that Paul is a prisoner awaiting trial in Rome, and we would like to know whether he was condemned or acquitted. But Luke does not tell us.

The reason for this is clear: the main character in the book of Acts is not the Twelve, or the Seven, or Paul. The protagonist of the second work by Luke is the Holy Spirit. Indeed, many have suggested that the title of the book should be "The Acts of the Holy Spirit" rather than "The Acts of the Apostles."

It is important to remember that in ancient times most books did not have a title, and if they did, the title was a reference not to the entire contents of the book, but rather to the beginning. Thus, a book that today we might call *A History of the United States*, which would cover the entirety of U.S. history, might be titled, according to ancient practice, *A History of the First Spanish Settlement in St. Au-*

gustine. This would be the case even if the description of that first settlement made up only part of the first chapter. Thus, whoever gave the book of Acts the title "The Acts of the Apostles" did not mean thereby that the book dealt only — or even mostly — with the apostles and what they did, but rather that the book began by telling the acts of the apostles.

While the Gospel of Luke focuses more on the acts and teachings of Jesus, and Acts turns its attention mostly to the work of the Holy Spirit in the church, the two books are not contrasting but are actually woven together. In the Gospel, while Jesus is present, it is through him that one sees the work of the Holy Spirit; and in Acts, after Jesus is "taken above," it is through the Spirit that one sees the work of Jesus. The close connection between these two books is clear in the beginning of the Gospel, where it is the Spirit who leads Simeon to acknowledge Jesus.

Thus, the best way for us to clarify what Luke says about who the Spirit is and how the Spirit works may well be to quickly review the entire book of Acts, where the activity of the Spirit is even more prominent than it is in the Gospel of Luke.

After the prologue addressing the book to Theophilus, where Luke clarifies the relationship between his two books, he returns to the subject of the Ascension, which appeared at the end of his Gospel. But here he adds a conversation between Jesus and his disciples that does not appear in the Gospel. The disciples ask Jesus, "Lord, is this the time when you will restore the kingdom to Israel?" (Acts 1:6). To this Jesus responds,

> It is not for you to know the times or periods that the Father has set by his own authority. But you will receive power when the Holy Spirit has come upon you; and you will be my witnesses in Jerusalem, in all Judea and Samaria, and to the ends of the earth. (Acts 1:7-8)

These words are well-known and often repeated for two reasons: first, because it is here that Jesus promises the Spirit to his disciples; and second, because it is a kind of outline for the rest of the book. We will return to this latter point. But at present it is important for us to note something we frequently miss or do not interpret correctly. This has to do with the very question of the disciples and Jesus' answer. From my earliest days, whenever I heard preaching on this dialogue, I was told that it shows that the disciples do not understand the message of Jesus, because they are preoccupied with the restoration of the kingdom, and that this is why Jesus refuses to answer their question.

But this is not what the text says. Jesus does not criticize the disciples for believing that the kingdom is to be restored, but rather for asking about the time when this will happen: "It is not for you to know the times or periods that the Father has set by his own authority." This is fundamentally important to understanding the function of the Spirit. Throughout the ages, and even to this day, there have been and still are those who claim that the Holy Spirit has told them "the times or periods" of God's plan. Thus they tell us, for example, that the Spirit has given them a new understanding of Scripture, and that thereby they are able to calculate and to foretell exactly the time when the Lord shall return. In so doing, they are contradicting the clear words of Jesus: "It is not for you to know the times or periods."

The fact is that Jesus does not tell the disciples that they should not be thinking about the restoration of the kingdom. Returning to what was said above about the matter of typology, it is clear that the Davidic kingdom is a type or figure of the reign of God, and that therefore Jesus did come to restore and to complete the kingdom — even though that kingdom may not be of this world, and even though the new restored Israel includes people from every tribe and nation.

What Jesus does add — and this must be stressed — is the purpose of the gift of the Spirit. The promise of that gift begins with the word *but*: "But you will receive power when the Holy Spirit has come upon you." In other words, the Spirit is not to tell us the times or the periods, but the Spirit will come. And the purpose of the outpouring of the Spirit is not to know the hidden secrets of God, but rather to give witness to Jesus: "And you will be my witnesses. . . ."

In the story of the Pentecost in chapter 2, the promise begins to be fulfilled in the gift of the Spirit. But there is still another element that remains incomplete: the promise that the disciples will be witnesses "to the ends of the earth" — a promise that will remain for future generations. The passage is so well-known that many of us know it by heart. But there is an important feature of the Pentecost that helps us understand the work of the Spirit both in Acts and in the life of the church: the tongues being spoken. If the purpose of the Spirit at Pentecost was to make it possible for all those present to understand what the disciples were saying, there were two options: one of them was to make all understand the Aramaic that the disciples spoke; the other was to make all understand in their own tongues. This would mean that the Romans would have heard in Latin, the Arabs in Arabic, the Egyptians in Coptic, and so on. The result would seem to be the same no matter what option the Spirit chose, for all would have been able to understand the message of the disciples. But in terms of the practical life of the church, each of these two options would lead in different directions.

If the Spirit decided that all were to understand the language of the disciples, the inevitable consequence would be that from that time on, the language, culture, and customs of the disciples would be normative in the life of the church. In order to be a leader in that church, it would be necessary to speak the tongue of the disciples, who therefore would also remain in control.

But if, on the other hand, the Spirit made each understand

in his or her own tongue, this means that all languages and all cultures could be vehicles for the gospel. It also means that quite soon the positions of leadership would be passed on to people of other languages and cultures. It is not necessary to insist much on this second option as the one chosen, for the entire history told in Acts, and the history of the church from then on in its best times, has been precisely that history of crossing borders, of becoming incarnate in new peoples and cultures.

What are the other consequences of this proclamation of the gospel in each one's tongue? One is that control will no longer be in the hands of the first disciples, for each church will transcend the limits of their reach — cultural limits as well as geographical ones. In chapter 6 of Acts, we already see something of this: there is a disagreement within the church having to do with questions of culture. There is murmuring against the apostles, and they decide that seven new leaders are to be named who must be "full of the Spirit and of wisdom" (v. 3). It is interesting to note that all those chosen have Greek names. In chapters 7 and 8, two of those leaders come to occupy the center of the stage. The first of them is Stephen, about whom Luke repeats that he was a man "full of faith and the Holy Spirit" (Acts 6:5). According to what the apostles had decided, Stephen was supposed to administer, but not to preach. And yet it is Stephen who preaches the longest sermon in the entire book of Acts! The second of those leaders who for a moment comes to occupy the center of action is Philip, who preaches first to the Samaritans in Samaria, and then to the Ethiopian eunuch on the road from Jerusalem to Gaza.

Luke tells us that in Samaria many were converted, and the church in Jerusalem sent Peter and John, who imposed their hands on those who had been baptized, and they received the Holy Spirit. Clearly, the apostles still have the power that was given to them at Pentecost. But what happens when they use that power is that the

Samaritans also receive the Holy Spirit. These new converts who were not in Jerusalem on the day of Pentecost now have their own Pentecost, and they receive the same power that the first disciples received before them. True, Peter and John have the power of laying on hands so that people may receive the Spirit; but now that these people also have the Spirit, they are no longer dependent on Peter and John, for they too have the same power. We should note that from this moment on, John disappears from the narrative, and Peter fades away as the church crosses new frontiers and new leaders appear.

★   ★   ★

It would be possible to continue this story by reviewing the entire book of Acts. But what is clear is that soon there are churches and leaders of different cultural backgrounds — churches and leaders that, even while they keep their ties with the church in Jerusalem and with the first disciples, are not subject to them: the eunuch who returns to Ethiopia with the message of the gospel; the Roman Cornelius, who takes it to his Gentile household; Lydia, the seller of purple; the jailer at Philippi; and, the most famous of all, Saul of Tarsus.

Now we can see why the Spirit made all understand in their own tongues at Pentecost: because the power that the Spirit gives is not power to be hoarded, but power to be shared. What the Spirit does at Pentecost is to give the first disciples the power to give similar power to those who listen to them — Parthians, Medes, Elamites, and so forth.

This is quite different from what many have claimed throughout history. It is very different from the claim to rule the entire church simply by being Peter's successor. It is also very different from the power that today some self-appointed "apostles" claim and then employ, not to share their power with others, but to control, to claim to be superior to the rest of the church. Let it be said in passing that these are people whom Paul would sarcastically call "super-apostles" (2 Cor. 11:5).

What is more, in the face of any supposed super-apostle, in the face of any hierarchy that claims to be able to control the Spirit, and in the face of our own inclination to try to domesticate the Spirit, it is important to stress that the Spirit is always free and sovereign. We like to systematize everything, to have a place for everything, and too often we seek to do the same with the Holy Spirit. This may be seen when we consider the matter of the order of water baptism and the baptism of the Spirit. People try to systematize things and to tell us which should happen first, and how. But this is not what Luke does. In Acts 2:38, Peter seems to take for granted that the gift of the Spirit is an almost automatic consequence of conversion and baptism: "Repent, and be baptized every one of you in the name of Jesus Christ so that your sins may be forgiven; and you will receive the gift of the Holy Spirit." But in Acts 9:17-18, after Saul's experience on the way to Damascus, Ananias tells him that he has been sent so that Saul may recover his sight and be full of the Holy Spirit; Ananias makes no mention of baptism. In Acts 10, in the home of Cornelius, and then in Acts 11, before the church in Jerusalem, Peter is a witness to instances in which the Holy Spirit is received before baptism. What these different examples show us is that the Holy Spirit is never under the control of the believers or of the church. So, rather than trying to systematize and regulate the work of the Spirit, we should be constantly open to God's surprising acts, as were those who had gone with Peter to the home of Cornelius, and "were astounded that the gift of the Holy Spirit had been poured out even on the Gentiles" (Acts 10:45).

Returning then to the passage regarding the gift of the Spirit at Pentecost, one can say that just as the quotation from Isaiah in

Luke 4 is an indication of what will follow in the rest of the Gospel, so the quotation from Joel in Acts 2 is an indication of what the rest of the book will show. And this is that the Spirit respects no privilege. The essence of Joel's message is that the Spirit will be poured out on "all flesh," and then he gives several concrete examples: sons and daughters, young and old, male and female servants. The Spirit comes not to create new hierarchies, but to create a community that will be a foretaste of the reign of God, and in which all will equally share the same power.

After setting the foundation for the mission of the Spirit in Acts 2, Luke goes on with his narrative, in which the main actor is always the Spirit — so constantly that if we sought to say and to explain all that Luke says about the Spirit, we would have to reread the entire book of Acts. For instance, we would have to deal with how in Acts 5 the great sin of Ananias and Sapphira is to have lied to the Holy Spirit, how in Acts 8 the Spirit carries Philip away after he baptizes the Ethiopian eunuch, how in Acts 13 the Spirit tells the believers to set aside Barnabas and Saul, how in Acts 11 and Acts 21 the Spirit is revealed in the prophet Agabus, and so on.

But what is crucial for us to realize is not only the importance the Spirit has in Luke's work, but also the fact that the very structure of that work reminds us that the Spirit is still active. As we saw at the beginning, Luke's work is incomplete. The narrative simply stops, but the story of the acts of the Spirit, or of the acts of Jesus through the Spirit, goes on.

History can be studied or written out of mere antiquarian curiosity, but it can also be written and read because one is aware that the story still continues. In this case, history becomes for us not mere information, but also a calling, a challenge, an invitation. As we finish reading Luke's work, it seems clear that, while the acts of the apostles have ended, the acts of the Spirit are still going on.

The promise in Acts 1:8 has been fulfilled only in part, for we have still not been witnesses "to the ends of the earth." There are still many waiting to hear the message and to see it at work, and they are not only in faraway lands, but also in our own lands, in our backyards, on the other side of our fence. If that promise made in Acts 1:8 is the outline of the story that Luke is telling us, he did well in not finishing this story. He did well because the promise and the calling are still valid. Because to this day we still have not been witnesses "to the ends of the earth." Because still today, in order to be such witnesses, we must count on the power of the Holy Spirit.

Luke's Open Invitation

AS WE HAVE SEEN, Luke's two-volume work was left unfinished. It is first of all unfinished in the geographical sense. In Acts 1:8 the disciples were told that they were to be witnesses to Jesus beginning in Jerusalem, and eventually to the ends of the earth. But at the end of the book their witness has reached no farther than Rome, so the promise of Acts 1:8 has barely begun to be fulfilled. And Luke's work is also unfinished in a chronological sense, for at the end Paul is awaiting trial in Rome, and nothing is said about the outcome of that trial, or the rest of Paul's life, or whatever became of Peter, John, and the rest.

As we noted earlier, we may look at an unfinished work in one of two ways. From a certain perspective, the work is defective. After engaging our interest, it fails to satisfy our curiosity. After all, a good story must have a beginning and an end. Any student of literature and any prospective novelist know that a good plot, after engaging the reader, comes to a point of crisis, which then is resolved in the denouement of the story.

Any chronicler knows that it is helpful to provide some of the background of the story to be told. If it is a chronicle of the reign of Charles V, it may well begin with a word about his grandparents, Isabella and Ferdinand, and about his parents, Joanna the

Mad and Philip the Fair. At the beginning of the Gospel of Luke there is something similar to that: we are told about Elizabeth's conception, the birth of John the Baptist, the genealogy of Jesus, and then the Annunciation.

But any chronicler also knows that the story must be carried on to its proper end. The story of the reign of Charles V must continue at least to the point of his abdication, or perhaps even to his death. If such a story ends at the point where Charles is preparing to deal with Luther or with the Turks, it is defective; the chronicler has left it incomplete. Yet this is precisely what Luke does! Paul has suffered countless vicissitudes. He has been shipwrecked. He has finally made it to Rome. He is awaiting trial before Caesar. And then — nothing!

However, from a different perspective, an unfinished story may have a purpose — and Luke's certainly does! If we look closely, we realize that it has a clear point of crisis and a clear resolution. The entire story reaches its climax at the cross — at the point where the confrontation between Jesus and the forces of evil that are present throughout the story comes to its culmination. And the denouement comes at the Resurrection, as in the other Gospels. Not even death could hold the son of Mary. Luke agrees with the other Evangelists that, as the hymn joyfully proclaims, the victory is won!

But, unlike the other Evangelists, Luke is not content with ending the story there. His Gospel goes on to tell us of the Ascension, and in his second volume he picks up the story at that juncture. This is probably the most salient point about the uniqueness of Luke's witness: he is not just telling his readers about something that took place in Judea years ago; he is also telling Theophilus and all his readers throughout the centuries that the story goes on. This does not mean that the events in Judea are less important. But it does mean that their importance must be seen and experienced by people in many different contexts, times, and places — by Parthians, Medes, and Phrygians, by people in Jerusalem, and in all of Judea, and in Samaria, and to the ends of the earth, by people in lands whose existence was unknown to Luke himself, people speaking a multitude of languages far beyond those represented at Pentecost, using technologies that would have baffled Luke.

In telling his story and leaving it unfinished, Luke is inviting his readers to be part of it, to join the throng. We could read a chronicle about Charles V, be fascinated by it, and then move on to other things. But we cannot let go of Luke's story that easily. We cannot let it go, among other reasons, precisely because it does not end. It extends through time and geography to reach us, no matter where or when that may be. If this were simply a story about the past, it would be appropriate to write, at the conclusion of Acts 28, as at the conclusion of a film, "The End." But since the story is unfinished, it is more appropriate to conclude it with "RSVP," like an invitation that awaits a response. This is what Luke demands from us: not satisfied curiosity about the past, but a response here and now. RSVP!